Becoming a Catechist

Ways To Outfox Teenage Skepticism

WILLIAM J. O'MALLEY, S.J.

paulist press   *new york/new jersey*

Library of Congress Cataloging-in-Publication Data

O'Malley, William J., 1931–
     Becoming a catechist: Ways to Outfox Teenage Skepticism/by William J. O'Malley.
          p.   cm.
     ISBN 0-8091-3323-7
     1. Catechists. 2. Catechetics—Catholic   Church. 3. Catholic Church—Education.   I. Title.
BX1918.048   1992
268′.3—dc20   92-14192
                                                                      CIP

Published by Paulist Press
997 Macarthur Boulevard
Mahwah, New Jersey 07430

Printed and bound in the
United States of America

Contents

For
MARIANNE CONWAY
and
BARBARA REYNOLDS

Introduction: The High Art of Religious Seduction

"Remember, I am sending you out like sheep among wolves. You must be cunning as serpents and yet as harmless as doves."

—Matthew 10:16

Expectations

In my second year teaching after ordination, I held the uncoveted eminence of theology chair in my high school. I was new, eager, and no one else would take it. At one faculty council meeting, I said (agitatedly), "If I can't get seniors to face the God questions *now,* they're gonna go off to some secular college next year and some atheist prof is gonna make pretzels out of them!" Art Inguaggiato, the history chair, turned a somewhat bemused face at me and said, "Who the hell are you? God?" Well, I fumed out of there. "That arrogant, that . . . who the . . . ?" Then I was pole-axed by an epiphany: "My God, he's *right!*" Humbling to my fired-up sense of mission, but true.

"Paul plants. Apollos waters. God gives the increase." In teaching theology, we are at first not even planters. Our primary job (which we often neglect) is to till the soil first; unless we do, our seed falls on rock-solid ground. Our initial task is *pre*-evangelization: to humanize them *before* we attempt to Christianize them. Even then, we are no more than matchmakers, trying to make God—and religion—appealing enough to our students that they will consider embracing them, perhaps even freely choose them for their own. Theology, belief, and religion are all gifts which can be refused. But God can draw people to him by any means he chooses, and at any time.

Since that faculty council meeting, I've lowered my expectations considerably. I no longer hope (against reality) to send out one hundred and fifty hot-eyed apostles every year. After all, Jesus died a failure as a teacher: one of his seminarians turned him in; his favorite denied knowing him, three times in one night; at the first sign of serious opposition, they all hiked up their skirts and skedaddled. After three years, twenty-four hours a day, with the greatest Teacher who ever lived, after the lacerating trauma of the crucifixion, the stupefying experience of the resurrection, and a month more of instruction, the *very* last question they asked was: "Are you going to restore the kingdom to Israel *now?*" They still yearned to put their tushes on those golden thrones. Jesus must have said, "Where the hell is that elevator?"

I wouldn't mind one or two hot-eyed apostles; I wouldn't mind one or two vocations. But I don't expect them. I don't even expect many to be overly interested in religion. But I do expect them to be at least a little *less dis*interested, a little less smugly certain that all they hear on the Tube and through the Walkman and from the stereo are the real Holy Writ. I'm pleased if a few in each class suspect that I am—and have—something valuable, something they might like to have, too.

And every year I do find that, yes, I did make a difference, at least a little. For instance, just yesterday, a boy who consistently, savagely insisted that homosexuals *chose* to be homosexuals, sat nodding agreement when I said that simply wasn't true. A survey question I gave earlier in the year (no credit, just stirring the sludge before class) was: "In a race, say at summer camp, a handicapped person should be given a head start." (The question is cunningly seeded in before we have to discuss racism, sexism, etc.) Maybe two in any given class say yes in that first fly-by; all the rest violently disapprove, with all kinds of alibis: "He'll think life is like that; he'll feel condescended to; etc." But just yesterday, when we finally got to racism, I asked the question again, and about ten in each class said yes. Not exactly a mob surging toward Billy Graham to proclaim Jesus their personal savior, but as Tybalt said, " 'Twill do."

One of the biggest triumphs I ever had wouldn't look like such to someone outside the field. One really terrific senior had good-naturedly battered me every time I said that two people aren't two animals, that there isn't just a physical encounter in human sex but also a psychological encounter, and if there isn't one, the two people degrade one another. "Come *on!*" Jimmy said, every time. "If she wants it as much as you do, what's wrong?" And I always countered, "If she came to you on her knees and pleaded with you to make her your slave [Jimmy is black], to tie her to your plow and beat her, would that make it moral?" Every time. You could have scripted it. But the last day of class, Jimmy came up to the desk, hooked his arm around my neck, and said, "Pops, we both know you're right. But I just can't give it up." As with the rich young man, that was as far as Jimmy was able to go *for the moment*. But that was a long step forward.

My patron saint as a teacher is Annie Sullivan. How

many weeks did she draw signs in Helen Keller's uncomprehending hands. Not only that, but Helen kept batting her
hands away! Yet Annie had faith—in Helen and in herself.
She *knew* that someday Helen was going to bump into that
pump—or into something—and say, "Oh, my God! I'm not
alone!" Same with me and Jimmy.

We can't sell faith if we don't have it ourselves.

Theology/Belief/Religion

Let's be rid—with all due speed—of the words
"religion class" and "religious education." They're the
wrong words.

Theology is what you *know* about the God questions;
belief is what you *accept* of what you know; and religion is
what you *do* about what you accept. They are quite separable and distinct.

Theology is what you know. Saints flunked courses in
theology with embarrassing frequency; atheists can get A's
in theology. Voltaire *knew* a great deal more about Catholicism than Joan of Arc. Had she known more, she might have
stayed home.

Belief (faith) is what you accept of what you know. I
can know, for instance, that the church says using artificial
means of birth control is sinful, but I could personally not
accept that as true when considered with all the other things
I know about biology, people, and God.

Religion is what you do about what you accept. I can
accept, for instance, that what the church says about abortion being premeditated homicide is objectively true, but
when I or my daughter or girlfriend gets pregnant, I might
do something contrary to what I genuinely believe. I may
honestly believe there is a God who gave me life, but I can
mean-spiritedly take the gift and never say thanks.

Theology and belief and religion are *not* the same thing.

The *only* thing we can teach (test, grade) is theology. We cannot teach belief and religion; we can only "sell" them, try to make them attractive to *this* audience. If you ask for an opinion and the student gives his or her opinion, you can't take off any points. If I ask, "What do you think of me?" and a student writes, "I think you're an arrogant blowhard," he or she gets full grades. They answered my question. If I ask their *reasoning* for their opinion, ah, that's another story. But I can't grade their opinions, only comment on them, usually—like "Jeopardy"—making sure I put my comment in the form of a question. And the only way you can fail religion is to go to hell.

P.T. Barnum and the Catechetical Quest

Unlike any other department—history, math, English —we are not just in the business of imparting information and broadening horizons. We are in the business of at least trying to elicit *acceptance,* to change basic attitudes toward what is important in life, to affect our students' behavior. Other teachers can be quite content if students just re- member the data till the exam and perhaps find some of it useful later. We are trying to convince them to *interiorize* what we teach. In a single word, our object is *conversion.*

The most self-defeating error any catechist can make is to presume that his or her students *have been* converted. Except for the very rare few, they have not. They are good kids, friendly, fun to be with, and they have been baptized, but they have not gone through the soul-searing process of conversion, nor is it likely that they will go through it while they're with you. The best you can hope for is that many will at least begin to suspect, like Helen Keller, that reality might be one helluva lot bigger than they'd ever suspected. The conversion part will have to be triggered by some event later in life, and the process will between the individual student and God. Remember: matchmakers.

In order to do that, we need to take a lot more lessons from Phineas T. Barnum and the maestros of Madison Avenue than we do from *The New Universal Catechism.* (If that be heresy, I'm ready for the secular arm.) Unlike the various directives given us from the official church, salesfolk spend megabillions and countless hours trying to create a *need* within the potential buyer *before* they offer the product.

That requires several considerations catechists have not frequently considered, judging only from the results. It means having a very good idea just where the audience *is:* their receptivities and especially their resistances. Therefore, constantly give them surveys and questionnaires which you pay close attention to but don't grade (so they're not just giving you "your" answer for the point, even though they believe otherwise). Start every class with ten statements that reflect the matter of the class: "Most people on welfare cheat": agree or disagree. Count the hands and record them; keep them and compare them year to year. But *don't* correct the "wrong" opinions; that's what the class is going to try to do. This is just the "hook."

And selling belief means *adapting* not only our message but our methods to the mind-set we find. It also means that we have to *pre*-evangelize them—a process many people in the business speak of and yet continue to demand textbooks which from day one "scream Catholic." It's simply not possible to do both at once.

Such a catechesis flies in the face of everything we know about salesmanship—to say nothing of the methods of Jesus. For generations, our catechesis has tried to make them Catholics *before* they are Christians, Christians before we are sure they are even theists, and believers before we've even taught them how to think. That completely reverses the *psychology of conversion.* Before, we waded right in there and gave them the whole ball of wax: *Filioque,* the virgin birth, infallibility, etc.—all the doctrines which *separate* Christians—before we showed them what all Christians believe. We simply assumed that, if they come from Catholic families, they must believe in God. Most students seem to "accept" that there must be "some kind of God," but most have only the vaguest idea of who that God might be or any kind of meaningful relationship with God, and only the barest few think that God or the God questions are in any genuine sense important—except for the test.

But we want more than the test. We hope for conversion.

Barnum not only knew the audience and created a need before he offered the product, but he also spent a great deal of time simply getting the audience's attention. Therefore, we have to spend *at least* as much time intriguing or irritating or puzzling them into alertness and engagement with the topic as we spend on learning the matter we have to teach. (Surely, anyone who merely goes in and outlines the text won't last long. That's what *they* should do, and on their own time.)

Helpful hint: A few years ago, a book came out called *To Teach as Jesus Did,* which then proceeded at length to show precisely how Jesus did *not* teach. He did not spin out doctrines; he did not theologize. He always started with a *story*. Believe me, if TV has left us nothing else, it has left us with the human desire for stories. Never begin right on the topic; always begin from a distance, blind-side them. When Jesus was asked who was the greatest in the kingdom, what did he do? He put a child in front of them. Puzzle, intrigue, irritate. Then maybe they're ready for your pitch. Plow before you sow.

Another skill the Madison Avenue pitchpeople have is their willingness to repeat. How many times does a given ad play in a day? "Nobody really listens." And yet you can repeat all the words, and when you go to the drugstore you reach for Bayer, at a buck more than generic, even though they're both exactly the same by government order. You don't want to say the same thing every day, but don't be afraid to bring up the subject again (think of Jimmy and casual sex). Maybe *this* time just one more will really *hear* you for the first time.

With an audience of skeptics, it is *not* enough merely to say "it's a commandment" or "the church says." You have to prove whatever your pitch by *reason;* not too many textbooks do that. They quote Vatican II at students who don't give two hoots for Vatican II; might as well be appealing to the authority of the Tooth Fairy. That means you have to pretty much reason each particular lesson out for yourself, bringing to bear on this truth everything you know not only from theology but from psychology, sociology, chemistry, physics, paleontology, literature: the works. Your liberal education is about to pay off!

Finally, their convictions will depend very heavily on *your* conviction. You have to have internalized for yourself all that you claim to believe about morality, the sacraments, the church. If you're just going in to "teach the matter," like a salesperson hawking a product he or she is not personally committed to and doesn't know right down to the roots, you will fail. Clare Boothe Luce said that when she was thinking of converting (and that's the business we're in), she looked at Catholics, especially seminarians, and said to herself, "You say you have the truth. Well, the truth should set you free, give you joy. Can I *see* your freedom? Can I *feel* your joy?"

Nifty question.

1

Understanding Understanding

"Rains came down, floods rose, gales blew and hurled themselves against the house, and it did not fall. It was founded on rock."

—Matthew 7:25

One day early on in my teaching, I got a lesson from a student that changed my whole understanding of my task as a teacher of theology and seducer to belief and religion. Oddly, it was in a junior English class. We were doing a poem by Amy Lowell called "Wind and Silver."

Greatly shining
The Autumn moon floats in the thin sky
And the fishponds shake their backs
    and flash their dragon scales
As she passes over them.
            —Amy Lowell (1874–1925)

I explained that, even with the metaphor comparing the light off the wavelets to dragon scales and the personification of the moon, it was just a simple picture; no great

11

probing of the human experience. A hand shot up: "I've got a different interpretation." I said that was fine, provided the evidence from the poem backed up the opinion; a poem's not a Rorschach test. "I think it's about a U-2 flight over Red China." I gaped; where was his evidence? "It's right there: 'dragon scales.' " This was gonna be a tough nut; you've just taken two words and spun out your own poem. "That's your opinion." I tried sarcasm: why couldn't it be a U-2 flight over medieval England; they had dragons, too. "That's your opinion." My teeth fused, but I knew I had him: "Look at the bottom of the *poem!*" I sort of shouted. "She was *dead!* There were *no* U-2's! There *was* no Red China!" But his face was smug as marble: "That's your opinion."

One can't stress this too much: THE most difficult task of being a teacher who deals not merely in facts and data but in converting opinions is confronting: "MY OPINION'S AS GOOD AS ANYBODY ELSE'S!" No, your opinion is *only* as good as the evidence that backs it up. Your opinion about physics is not as good as Albert Einstein's, and your opinion of a movie is not as good as an experienced actor's or director's. Even every first-year teacher has confronted it: "Do you want what we really think or *your* opinion?"

Part of it is caused by an unfocused resentment that, no matter how new the teacher is, the teacher knows *more* than the students do. They don't want to be one-upped just because you've read *books,* especially the kids who think street-smart is the only real smart. Face it down, every time. First, "If we come to a line in scripture or 'Hamlet,' and we have a difference of opinion about an interpretation, nine times out of ten I'll be right. Not every time, but most times." Growls, sneers. "The reason is that I've studied it more, read more of other people's interpretations, mulled it over and come to a pretty trustworthy conclusion." Growls, sneers. "*But* if I come to one of your dances (or games or whatever you know less about than they) and say the music sounds like exploding boilers, and you say the band is very good, nine times out of ten, *you'll* be right." Smug smiles of agreement. "Because you know more about it than I do."

Part of the smug conviction that "My opinion's as good as anybody else's" is the holder's conviction that the opinion actually *is* his or her own. But except for areas in which they have a great deal more experience (which are few, like sports or rock music), their opinions have almost every time come "off the rack" from their parents, the media, their pals. They are opinions, to be sure, and they are "theirs," but they are uninformed opinions, without any substantial evidence other than hearsay, and thus not worth the breath that's wasted on them.

In my experience, in every class of thirty or so, there will almost inevitably (and painfully) lurk three or four— or in a bad year, five—students who simply will *not* relent to even the most painstakingly supported statements. Most often they will be neither the brightest nor the dullest students, but those who have to prove (usually against their own painful inner convictions) that they are *not* among the duller and they *are* among the smarter—even if they are uninformed. (If they persist, it is a good idea to sit down with them one-on-one, where they have no need to shore up a shaky reputation in front of an audience.)

Part of that particular difficulty is that they simply don't want to lose. That can at least be challenged by: "Have you ever argued with your parents and suddenly realized, 'My God! They're *right'*—and yet you kept *on* arguing? Why? Because you don't want to find the truth. You want to *win*. Or at least not *appear* to lose. And yet the longer you argue with thin air for evidence, the bigger fool you make of yourself."

That unbending truculence is also often caused by the

fact that the teacher is in fact calling into question the credibility of the students' own parents, who have stoutly defended such certitudes as homosexuals freely choose to be gay and most people on welfare cheat. It's difficult to admit I am wrong, but it is even more difficult to admit my *father* is wrong. But that is the whole function of adolescence: to critique all the messages that parents and media have taped on their Superegos, against objective reality, to see which ones stand up and which don't.

A further reason—most especially when you challenge their unquestioned certitudes about sex—is that, if they ever admitted that what you say is true, based solely on objective evidence and rigorous reasoning, they'd have to give up something they like very, very much.

The one all-purpose weapon a teacher has to bring to class every day is: "Where's your *evidence?*" Very often it will be as thin as, "I know this guy who . . ." or "Everybody knows that . . ." Conversely, don't think *you* can get away with an assertion like, "Well, the church *says* . . ." or "There's a commandment . . ."

This incessant battle with courageous ignorance takes a great deal of *patience* over a very long haul. And it takes a great deal of *love,* because no one likes a messenger bringing bad news: you've made a mistake, and you have to go back to the first wrong turn and start over again. But unless a catechist uproots those obstacles/certitudes, *everything* else is building a house on sand. They will not even be able to *hear* a gospel that enjoins forgiveness, self-forgetfulness, and chastity, when they have been superbly brainwashed by the media—since before they could even think—to accept unquestioningly that the more things they have, the happier they'll be; to be self-absorbed in their looks, their possessions, and their achievements; and even the most admirable characters in the serials "get it" without paying.

The same is true about morality. Another variation on "my opinion's as good as anybody else's" is "morality changes from age to age and culture to culture." I don't know where the hell they get that, but for thirty years—through all kinds of changes from Eisenhower to Nixon to Bush—that conviction has been rock solid in both high school and college students. Therefore, another epistemological knot the teacher has to address—before *any* other teaching—is the difference between *objective* facts and *subjective* opinions.

It's undeniable that *subjective* morality has changed from age to age, but *objective* morality is rooted in *the natures of things,* which don't change from age to age. Rocks are still the same as they were three thousand years ago; so are carrots, bunnies, and human beings. Styles may change: curlicued wigs to flattop haircuts, bustles to bikinis. But what it means to be a good human being doesn't change. Perhaps cultures have debated over the humanity of blacks and Jews, but the humanity of blacks and Jews is not debatable. It's a fact as objectively unchallengeable as the spherical shape of the earth and the toxicity of cyanide. But the audience you will face as a catechist firmly believes that there is no difference between morality and "lifestyle."

What Validates Opinions?

Every year, every class—even in English class—I tell students that *the* most important statement I'm going to make all year is this: "The tree comes *to* me." It tells me what it *is* (categorizing) and how I can legitimately *use* it (evaluating). A human being is not merely an animal; it has a conscience. An animal is not a vegetable; it can feel pain. A vegetable is not a rock; it can feed people. Those are objec-

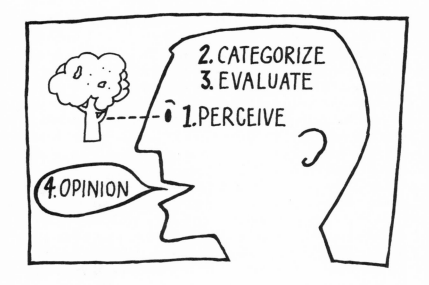

tive facts, no matter whether I like them or not or whether I'm aware of them or not.

The first step (*sine qua non*) is to *perceive* the data. If I'm blind, my opinion about color isn't worth listening to; if I study the data only cursorily, my opinion is swamp gas. (And isn't that how a great many students approach an essay or a reaction paper?) The second step is to *categorize* this new object with other objects of the same species, so I don't have to start from scratch with each new item I encounter. The third step is to *evaluate* this object and how I can legitimately use it. The fact that this object is a human being shows that I can't herd it as I can herd cattle; it has a greater dignity, simply because it is human. I can't throw a living dog into boiling water as I can a carrot, simply because the dog can feel pain. I can't lob food around the cafeteria as if it had no more *inherent* value than snowballs. Then I have a right to express an *opinion,* but it is wise to take a final fifth step and ask someone I trust to *critique* it. If I study the evidence and come to the conclusion that I've just seen a unicorn eating a lily, I'd like to get a second opinion. It could be a horse with an arrow in its forehead, and I'll look like a perfect fool.

We have to realize that, unlike any other teachers, as religious educators we are not only trying to impart knowledge and broaden horizons, we are trying to change *opinions.* If what we say about the purpose of human life is not *internalized,* we are wasting our time. If what we say is in direct contradiction to what our students firmly believe (and it is), then we have our work cut out for us.

All this may seem painfully obvious and simple to a new teacher who's just rarin' to get in there and dump Luke on them or have grand debates on morality. But if you don't force them to understand the rules of evidence, you might as well be speaking Mandarin. If you don't plow the soil first, you're planting your seeds on solid rock.

Reasoning

Every student thinks, in the sense that they all have ideas, mull opinions, worry a problem. But very few of them know how to *reason.* And yet that is the primary purpose of education: to learn how to reason with ever more complex data. The facts they cram and regurge they will never remember. We didn't. I haven't factored a quadratic equation in forty years, nor could I—even though I was a crackerjack at them in high school.

The problems our students will face haven't been invented yet. What teacher who taught me religious education forty years ago could have envisioned nuclear waste, a hole in the ozone, genetic engineering, wholesale abortion, the

Pill? What's more, many of the questions we want to become
real for students will not become real—nor will our answers—no matter how zealously we try. But later in their
lives, the problems very well may become important, but
they will have forgotten our handy answers. Then they'll
have to figure it out for themselves. Therefore, the *best*
thing we can teach—after we have shown the absolute importance of objective evidence and the difference between
objective fact and subjective opinion—is how to reason.

The reasoning process is rather easy to explain—even
though few teachers I know ever do it.

(1) Gather the data
(2) Sift out the most important data
(3) Put the data into some kind of logical sequence
(4) So you can draw a conclusion (opinion, thesis)
(5) And put it out to be critiqued

That is, quite simply, the scientific method, and it
should be applied as rigorously in theology as in physics.
What else do we ask students to do when they write essays:
(1) do research, much of which will later prove unusable;
(2) sift out the essentials; (3) write a logical outline; (4) lay
out the data in a progressive statement proving the thesis;
(5) submit it for a teacher's critique. What do we ask for in
lab reports? Same thing, although the outline is already laid
out like a recipe. What will they do when the boss asks their
best recommendation on the Smith account? Same thing.
What do you do when you're trying to solve a moral problem? Same thing. What do you do when you're trying to find
out if there's a God or not? Same thing: gather, sift, put into
logical sequence, draw a conclusion, and put it out to be
critiqued.

And yet I know very few teachers who actually, explicitly teach that—even though it is the *core* of education. And the results show that the students haven't learned that very well in many cases. Too many write without research or brainstorming, off the top of their heads, thus there's not much to sift; too many skip the outline, even though professionals have to outline, and if you demand an outline, too many will write the paper and then fake the outline; and how many of the misspelled words you circled turn up misspelled on the next paper? The only real writing is *re*writing.

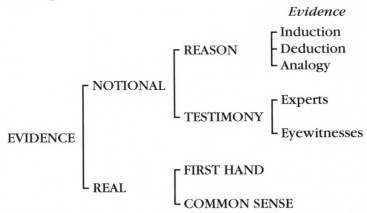

Evidence

```
                                              ┌ Induction
                          ┌ REASON          ┌─┤ Deduction
                          │                 │ └ Analogy
             ┌ NOTIONAL ──┤
             │            │                 ┌ Experts
             │            └ TESTIMONY ───────┤
EVIDENCE ────┤                              └ Eyewitnesses
             │
             │            ┌ FIRST HAND
             └ REAL ──────┤
                          └ COMMON SENSE
```

Notional evidence is second-hand, academic, *probable.* Real evidence is first-hand, experiential, *certain.*

Reason argues from data that are certain to conclusions that are, in varying degrees, probable. *Induction* argues from consistent patterns to generalizations: every time I put out a pan of water when the temperature is below thirty-two degrees, the water goes stiff; every time I drink five martinis, I regret it; every time I've seen people treat sex like a game, it's lost its importance to them. *Deduction* applies generalizations to new cases: every time I drink five martinis, I regret it; but this is my fifth martini; therefore: Ooops! *Anal-*

ogy tries to explain realities we do not understand in terms of realities we do understand. For instance, if an abortionist were out hunting and had left his glasses back in the cabin, can he fire at moving bushes even when he's not completely sure what's causing it, even though he hasn't seen another human being in days?

Expert testimony is trustworthy, provided the person is speaking in his or her field of expertise. Carl Sagan knows a great deal more about astronomy than I do, and I must bend to his scientific opinions, but when he starts talking about theology, he's talking about a subject he knows less about than I do. What's more, experts can often differ; otherwise, there would never be any occasions for debate. What the students must do is take both sides *as* the evidence, the data, and make as honest a judgment about the validity of one side or the other. *Eyewitness* testimony is trustworthy, but only to a point. Any detective will testify that people don't make very good eyewitnesses to crimes. I trust the astronauts' testimony that they really did land on the moon, even though the pictures could have been faked in a studio, simply because they have no reason to deceive me. I accept the existence of China, the fact that tables aren't solid but rather galaxies of particles, that prussic acid isn't good to drink—on someone else's testimony, despite the fact that I haven't experienced them. But the testimony of one or two eyewitnesses ("I know this guy on welfare who drives a Cadillac") is too thin.

Real knowledge is so highly probable that it verges on certainty (which only God can have undiluted). *First-hand experience* is the best evidence there is (even though it, too, is limited: this table *seems* unarguably solid, but it's not). Seeing is not believing; seeing is *knowing*. I believe God exists, but I know that this class is sitting out in front of me. The best way to answer the God questions, then, after all the notional knowledge has been gathered, is to come and see: to *meet* God, person-to-Person. *Common sense* is also close to certain. Although I have no direct knowledge of it, I'm pretty sure that the first floor of the school is still there, that each of the students I teach had two parents, one male and one female, that it's highly unlikely the world will end tomorrow.

Again, all this might seem banally simple and obvious. It certainly would have been to me thirty years ago when I came out to teach, armed with a master's thesis on Dostoevsky's vision of human nature. It was terrific. I got an A+. Having been condescended to in high school English, I was going to open up the world of *Crime and Punishment* to my lucky students. Disastrous. I was governed not by what the kids needed but by what I needed.

Thirty years of experience convince me that every teacher should teach these epistemological lessons *before* trying to teach anything else: "The tree comes *to* me"; the difference between objective fact and subjective opinion; one's opinion is only as good as the evidence that backs it up; opinions are only one's own when one gathers the data, sifts it, puts it into some kind of logical sequence, draws a conclusion, and puts it out to be critiqued. No matter that some teacher has taught it the previous year. *Repetitio est mater studiorum.* And very often when I teach it to a group of seniors, they are genuinely impressed—even though I had also taught them the exact same things as juniors. They just weren't ready then. Perhaps if students heard all this often enough, they might find out what education—even religious education—is for.

The Obstacles

Beginning—and veteran—teachers have always got to remember the obstacles that stand between our students and what we are trying to have them accept, and we have to have the students both see and *acknowledge* that the obstacles exist and get in the way of their seeing the truth, not just in religion but in all phases of life.

First, there are obstacles *inside* the students, all rooted in the self-absorption and inertia we inherited from our animal forebears, what we call original sin. Self-protection often gets between us and the objective truth, simply because acknowledging the truth makes us rethink, change priorities, go back to the first wrong turn and start over again. At the root of all these inner obstacles to seeing and doing the truth is fear of the cost. And anyone who believes that our gospel message doesn't cost has never truly heard the gospel message.

Second, there are obstacles programmed into us from *outside,* prejudices built up over years and years which hold that such-and-such opinion is certain and unchallengeable. The *media* give a palpably false view of human life to anyone open-eyed and with a wider perspective. The programs show a simplistic view of family life, business, police, doctors, lawyers; the commercials not only prejudice us to place an inordinate value on looks, bodies, possessions, but they turn greed into a virtue. (You will find that any critique whatever of capitalism is equivalent in many students' eyes to communism and anti-Americanism.) *Pop music* may be neutral as music, but most of it also has lyrics, and those lyrics express a particular point of view on human values. (Get copies of *Hit Parader,* et al., and photocopy at least the lyrics they're allowed to print. Show that there are, indeed, patterns: e.g., Baby, it's all over but let's do "it" just one more time, etc.) The whole *Playboy mystique,* which has spilled over to MTV, commercials, print ads, soap operas and sitcoms, has had a pervasive effect on our ability to look at sex objectively, rather than through the filters programmed into us all day, every day. The *church* itself is quite often an obstacle to its own message in the students' eyes: its liturgy doesn't seem to be a celebration, the members supply an endless stream of anecdotes showing that membership doesn't seem to make people any more generous or forgiving than non-members, its doctrines seem, to the students, to be nothing more than "all those rules" that try to crimp one's freedom. The everyday *school* experience also prejudices the young to feel that grades are what it's all about and thus, rather than learning how to reason with ever more complex data, they become expert in dodges ("Is this gonna be on the test? Can the matching items be used more than once? Can I have an extension?"). And all these—and more—prejudices against seeing and accepting the truth are aided and abetted by the students' *parents and peers,* accepting false opinions as unquestionably true.

Sort of makes you wish you'd stuck to English or history, right? But we have two inescapable realities: the kids we love and the gospel we profess. We are matchmakers. Our job is to bring the two together. But before we can do that, we have to clear away the obstacles: the resistances within our audience to seeing the truth which point to the Truth.

The very first job of evangelization is pre-evangelization.

2

Understanding God

> Jesus turned around, saw them following, and said,
> "What do you want?" They answered, "Rabbi . . .
> where do you live?" And Jesus replied, "Come and see."
> —John 1:38–39

The first problem in dealing with faith in God is not who—or even whether—God is, but what faith is. Invariably, the students I've taught have said that faith is "a blind leap in the dark." Even after I've hammered away again and again that faith is a *calculated risk,* they consistently answer "True" to "Faith is a blind leap in the dark," and when I give it as: "Faith is a _____ _____ ," they still fill the blanks with "blind leap." Do they even listen to me? Do they think I'm crazy?

A blind leap in the dark is sheer idiocy. If someone comes to your door and offers you five acres in Florida for $5,000, and you give that four-flusher a check, that's a blind leap in the dark. No, faith is what two people do when they decide to get married. They don't *know* it will work out; they're *betting* it will work out, based on the evidence of their previous relationship. It's a calculated risk, and the more calculation, the less risk. Just so, I don't *know* God exists; I'm *betting* God exists, based on a great deal of reasoning which shows that God's existence seems more probable than God's non-existence, and based on what I sincerely believe is my own first-hand experience of God.

But, contrary to what most students have learned in other classes than yours, there is a limit to left-brain analysis. They have been taught, apodictically, that physics is "certain," as are biology and chemistry. Those are the subjects you can really *trust.* On the contrary, Werner Heisenberg won the Nobel Prize in Physics sixty years ago for enunciating the Principle of *Un*certainty. That Nobel Prize was actually a testament to humility, to the limitations of the human mind when confronted with complex, objective reality. *All* our assertions about objective reality fall quite short of the realities themselves. And if there's uncertainty about physics, there sure as hell and taxes is uncertainty about theology.

Students resent uncertainty. They want guarantees, and they've been guaranteed guarantees since before they could understand what guarantees meant. And they expose that resentment when you threaten their certitudes. The *facts* they've been offered in science classes, even in Catholic schools, through well-meaning (but not Nobel winning) science teachers, seem to brook no uncertainty—Heisenberg notwithstanding.

So, after the second problem (belief in the supposedly infallible powers of the left brain) comes the third problem: Why is God even worth troubling oneself about? Surely one can get along quite well *without* God, thank you very much. The first response is that if—for the sake of argument—God does actually exist, then we owe God everything. God opened the door—a gift which (since we didn't yet exist) we could have done nothing to deserve. If that is true, then we owe God everything; we are indebted. (Ah, beware! Indebtedness and gratitude are guilt-provoking. They limit freedom. They also becloud the objective evidence.)

Death

But, ultimately, the God question is really a *me* question. If there is, in fact, no God, then the dubiousness of my ultimate worth is logically inescapable. It's easy, when the only reality you have ever acknowledged is Lilliput, to believe that some guys are *really* big. But then all of a sudden Gulliver shows up. And in acknowledging Gulliver's undeniable largeness, we automatically acknowledge our own smallness—which is not a pleasant fact to submit to. And in our case, the ultimate Gulliver is God, and the proximate Gulliver is death.

The kids you teach have been shielded from death. The only deaths they've been exposed to are on TV and movie screens, and they know that the actors are going to get up and collect their paychecks. In fact, psychologists have shown that small children can't tell the difference between the faked deaths on cop shows and the real deaths on the news. What's more, unlike the "good old days" on "The Waltons," people who are sick or dying aren't "there." They go to hospitals and nursing homes and die "properly," without intruding on the "really real": i.e., where I am. (Interesting to canvass your classes and find how many have actually been to a wake or to a nursing home.)

To most kids, death is a very, very long way off. Not true. In 1986, two million Americans died. Of those, 38,600 were infants under one year of age; 23,000 died in traffic accidents; 20,000 died in home accidents; 27,000 victims were younger than twenty-four, "before their time." I myself have helped concelebrate too many adolescent funeral masses.

You either see and accept the truth, or you live an illusion. Death is (1) inevitable, (2) unpredictable, (3) ultimate, at least as far as this life is concerned—and certainly ultimate if this life is the limit of our existence.

Accepting one's own real death is not just a macabre realization. It shows the value of time; it tells us what is ultimately important and what is not; it tells us what "salvation" really means. The students you teach have been told that Jesus died to save us from "sin." That is strange. I accept Jesus as my personal savior, but he hasn't prevented me from sinning, again and again. What Jesus saved us from, by his resurrection, is ultimate meaninglessness. As even Nietzsche admitted, anyone who has a *why* to live for can undergo almost any *how*. But if there is nothing but the crapstorm, then death, no one can find anything but a fleeting and quite unsatisfactory "why." We're all on the *Titanic,* and there's only one destination. Mother Teresa and mob hitmen will get the same reward: annihilation.

This is one reason teachers should broaden students' perspectives to understand that most of the people who share this planet with us—in Bangladesh, Ethiopia, Haiti, Chad, Afghanistan, Cambodia—do not have what our students consider essentials: wall-to-wall carpeting, washer-dryers, stereos, cars. Food. Clothing. Shelter. Most people on this planet are more closely acquainted with Sisyphus than with Pollyanna. (That is the only serious reason I can find to study world hunger: to encourage a sense of gratitude and *noblesse oblige.*)

Atheism

Especially many very bright students make facile atheists, without having studied the question (gather, sift, etc.)

very deeply. Partly it seems to show that one is not naive; partly it is rebellion; partly it results from the fact that mass is undeniably boring. But one can't just toss God overboard without accepting the logically inescapable consequences.

In *The Dragons of Eden,* Carl Sagan (unwittingly, I suspect) shows the ultimate value of a human life in a godless universe. He compresses the history of the universe to a single year to show the relative value of time. Here is a selection of a few significant dates.

Jan 1		Big Bang
Sep 14		Formation of Earth
Dec 16		First worms
Dec 24		First dinosaurs
Dec 28		First flowers; dinosaurs extinct
Dec 31—	11:00 PM	First humans
	11:59 PM	Cave paintings in Europe
	11:59:51 PM	Invention of the alphabet
	11:59:59 PM	Renaissance in Europe

On that very scientific and objective scale, four hundred years is $\frac{1}{60}$ of a second. Then what is seventy years worth, objectively? What significance is the difference between seventy years and seventeen years? What is the objective value of your life if there is no other dimension to it but time, if you won't outlast time? No more importance than the wake of a ship.

Oh, we all feel quite significant inside our Lilliputian cocoons. But Death is Gulliver. When he shows up, we suddenly look quite small. Take a look at an earthrise and try to find how significant you are.

"Ah, but I'll make a difference. I'll live on in my children." Okay, take a best-case scenario: you win two Nobel Prizes, one for peace and one for literature; you win the gold swimming medal in the Olympics; you have ten children—each of them doctors, lawyers, college presidents, etc. But set your accomplishments against the accumulated accomplishments of the human race: the invention of fire, the conquests of Alexander, the plays of Shakespeare. Put your ten books in the Library of Congress. Does anybody remember Don Schollander? He won three gold medals in the Tokyo Olympics. A few years ago there was an earthquake in China in which 100,000 perished. Did you even know about it? Were they in any real sense "important"? And yet there were thousands of doctors, lawyers, college presidents, etc., and each one was somebody's son or daughter. Pfft! And half your DNA may live on in your children, but you won't be aware of it. You will have stopped being real.

Perhaps the atheists are right, but it is a grim alternative —and the *only* other alternative to God. If they are able, have the students read "Waiting for Godot" to find what life in a god-less universe is truly like.

The Highly Probable Existence of God

This is really the first question any theology course should begin with. If God *doesn't* exist, then all the theologies of all the religions of the world are just so much wasted time and paper, and there is no reason at all to study theology. Unfortunately, however, very young children aren't intellectually capable of the reasoning one needs to do to establish God's existence. Thus we consistently walk into class under the assumption that they believe in God. That's not always true. Therefore, this question should be faced as early as the teacher believes the students are ready for it.

We start with three presuppositions:

(1) Belief in the existence of God is an opinion, and thus, like any other opinion, an act of faith is only as good as

the *evidence* that backs it up, both notional evidence and real evidence. That's the "calculated" part.

(2) At the end of this exercise in reasoning, the best we can hope for is *a high degree of probability*. An act of faith is neither a blind leap in the dark nor an assent with complete certitude. That's the "risk" part.

(3) We are attempting to prove only that there is *a Mind Behind It All*. We are not here attempting to show that the power to whom we owe our existence is Yahweh, or Jesus, or Allah, or Buddha. Just that there is *some* power on whom the universe—and therefore each of us—depends for its existence. It is quite possible that the universe always existed, but there is no possibility that it created itself.

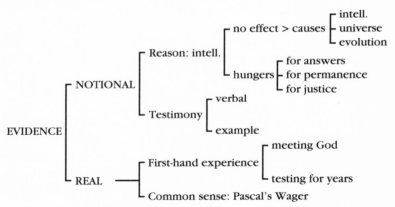

NOTIONAL EVIDENCE: Reason. Reason starts from evidence that is certain and argues to conclusions that are probable. So I start with my intelligence, which is an objective fact. But that intelligence tells me there can be no effect greater than the sum of its causes. If I put a pumpkin on the podium and it started belting out "Hey, Big Spender," you'd have to say, "There's a speaker inside, right?" because a pumpkin, all alone, is incapable of producing that effect.

You can't get blood out of stone, or a scream out of a carrot, or conscience out of the highest level animal we know.

I apply that principle—no effect can be greater than the sum of its causes—to my intelligence itself. How do we get intelligence out of non-intelligence? Perhaps intelligence was brought to us by space aliens, but no one could have looked at the primeval lava that covered the earth and said, "But of course! If we wait long enough, Shakespeare is *bound* to emerge from that."

I apply that principle to the universe itself, macro and micro. Everywhere I look, what do I find? Objects spinning on their axes. Not only that, but rotating around other objects, and that pair rotating around another in a cosmic dance of attraction and repulsion. Everywhere in the universe, the *same* dance! Everywhere, the *laws* of physics are the same. Isn't that coincidental, without a Choreographer? I could see how you could get *variety* out of an accident, but not *order*. How do you get law out of luck? To accept that, you'd have also to accept that if you dropped an atomic bomb on Mount Everest, there'd be at least a chance that the pieces would come down a working Disneyland. Or that if you got four tireless chaps at the four corners of a sheet containing the pieces of clock (which is a relatively simple mechanism compared to the universe) and they threw up the pieces an infinite number of times, sooner or later Part A would attach itself to Part B, and Part AB would attach itself to Part C, until sooner or later it would come down a working clock. Perhaps that's possible, but my brain can't handle it.

And what do I find when I go to the opposite end of the spectrum and analyze a droplet of ditch water under a microscope? The same damn dance! Isn't that coincidental? Every snowflake in Antarctica has exactly the same pattern, and yet no two are alike? Isn't that coincidental? Every year has the same pattern of seasons, and yet no two are alike. Isn't that coincidental? Every human being is built on the same model, and yet your DNA has never existed before and will never exist again. Isn't that coincidental? All that order and surprise, with no Mind Behind It All? *My* mind can't accept that. (Throughout this explanation, remind students of the chapter on epistemology: very often we don't want to see the truth because of what admitting the truth might cost us.)

I apply the principle of no effect greater than the sum of its causes to evolution. From this end, evolution looks like an incredible *plan*. But how do you get a plan without a Planner? To say it came about by a process of "natural selection" is, at best, a misuse of words. How can anything without intelligence make an intelligent "selection"? There has to be a mind and will for that. Atheists like Carl Sagan are thus forced to "give" intelligence to entities that don't have it. Thus: "One day, quite by accident, a molecule arose that was able to make crude copies of itself." Now that was one *helluva* clever molecule! Later in *Cosmos* he says that five hundred million years ago trilobites "stored crystals in their eyes to detect polarized light." How did those brainless trilobites even *know* there was light if they had no eyes? And how did they "figure out" how to store light crystals? *I* don't even know what they *are*.

Chance is very chancy. For instance, if I had ten cards, ace through ten, the chances of my pulling the ace are one in ten, of pulling ace-deuce one in one hundred. But the chance of my pulling ace-through-ten in order are about one in 3.6 billion—and that is a relatively simple sequence compared to all the cogs in the cosmic slot machine that had to fall into place in order to come up with us. Even Sagan admits that. The earth rotates at a thousand miles an hour at the equator; if it were any slower we'd all burn up. Isn't that lucky? The earth tilts at a 23-degree angle; if it weren't we'd have no seasons. Isn't that lucky? If the moon were, say, 50,000 miles away, we'd be inundated by tides twice a day, all mountains would be eroded, and the whole weather pattern would change. Isn't that lucky? If the crust of the earth were only ten *feet* thicker, there'd be no oxygen. Isn't that lucky?

For me, the human eye alone is evidence enough that there must be a Mind Behind It All. The eye even gave Darwin a bit of a problem, since he couldn't imagine how such an intricate instrument could have evolved by sheer chance. Think of it: it's a more perfect camera than any human could contrive, with a bellows and an *automatic* iris, which takes pictures—in three dimensions and in color—eighteen hours a day, and you never have to change the film! In fact, at times, when it is damaged, it will even repair itself! And it works even for retarded people.

My intelligence, which is, again, undeniable, also is the cause of undeniable "hungers," which no other species I know of has: the hunger for answers, the hunger for permanence, and the hunger for justice. I want to know why children have to suffer; I want to survive death; I want someone to make it up to people who are born maimed. But if there is no Mind Behind It All, if everything is just an accident, then there are no answers, we will not survive death, there are no reasons for suffering. Perhaps that's true, but then why are we the only species *cursed* with hungers for which there is no "food"? It's as if mindless evolution stumbled one cruel step too far and came up with a species which knows that everything it does is ultimately futile, that everything we do will be obliterated, and after a while no one will even remember we existed. No pig snoozing in maternal bliss in a ring of piglets has her dreams disturbed by the fact that one day all her babies will die. We do. If there is no food for those undeniable hungers, then it would be better to be a pig than to be a human being.

NOTIONAL: Testimony. As we saw, testimony is the shakiest of the sources of evidence, but it can at least be supportive of the notional evidence we've seen already. When I read the arguments of believers, they make sense to me. When I read the arguments of unbelievers, I come away burdened with the gloomy realization that everything I do is just killing time till time kills me.

Not that I'm saying that all atheists are suicidal or that all believers are joyful. Camus was most likely a saint; many of my co-religionists are mean-spirited Puritans. But when I see how belief fired the life of St. Teresa of Avila, a woman of prodigious penances and prodigious wit, I suspect she knows something a lot of people ought to know. The same is true of Thomas Becket, Thomas More, Tom Dooley. There is a radiance about people like Dorothy Day, Oscar Romero, Mother Teresa.

Perhaps the atheists are right, and we just have to find something to busy our days with till we die; whatever pleases you, that's justification enough. Well, I think I'd like to fill my days being like Mother Teresa.

When I was in "The Exorcist" and was invited onto "The Today Show," Barbara Walters leaned over to me during a commercial and whispered, "You're obviously an intelligent man. *How* can you be a priest?" And I said, "Because it gives me such joy." And she snapped (she really did!), "I don't know what that means." She makes well over a million dollars a year, but she doesn't know what joy means. That sure bolstered my belief.

REAL: First-Hand Experience. I truly believe that I have met the living God. One experience, when I was at the lowest point in my life and actually contemplating suicide, was an encounter which I can only describe as "drowning in light." When I emerged from it, after about two hours, I knew—for the first time in thirty-two years—that I was accepted, that I was a good man, and I never again needed anybody else to tell me. It has fueled everything I have done in the last twenty-eight years.

Here, I believe, the individual teacher is called upon to drop any pretense to shyness and forthrightly talk to students about his or her experiences with God. I have done it four or five times a year, and it has never failed to impress—and puzzle—kids more than anything else I've said all year.

What's more, I've tested out my belief by living that belief as close to full-throttle as I've been able for the last twenty-eight years, and I still can't find any other answer that's better.

Finally, common sense (Pascal's Wager) tells me that, if there are only two alternatives, and one of them is joyous and the other is desolating, and I have no way of knowing which is the truth, then I might as well take the joyous one. And I will never find out I was wrong! Carl Sagan isn't going to be on the other side of death thumbing his nose at me and saying, "I told you so, naive dolt!"

All of what for me is real evidence is, of course, for the student, only testimony—notional evidence. As we shall see in a later chapter, the religious education teacher has a fundamental task to set up situations where students at least have the opportunity to meet God for themselves. Then, like the first essential but disposable stage of a rocket, the notional evidence becomes no longer necessary.

What Is God Like?

It is important when studying other religions that we do not talk about "the Moslem's God" and "the Buddhist's

God." It is the same God, seen through the prisms of different cultures and mind-sets, like the elephant discovered by
the blind men in the Calcutta park. There is no time actually
to retail the differences in world religions here, but it is also
important in showing the "shortcomings" of each religion
that the teacher make clear that such-and-such picture of
God seems to be overbalanced or lacking when held up to
the God the *teacher* has experienced. Deists and Platonists
seem to picture God as too far away, too aloof, too transcendent for the God one has experienced as very close in
prayer. Pantheists and pagans seem to picture God as too
close, too locked into creation compared to the God one has
experienced. Yet each extreme can serve as a corrective
when my own ideas of God get overbalanced. The Deists
remind me that, although God seems like a "pal," he is still
inexpressibly holy and "other." The Pantheists remind me,
when I get lost in airy theologizing, that God is also right
there at my elbow, that I am surrounded by a world charged
with the grandeur of God.

In dealing with the Judaeo-Christian insights into the
nature and personality of God, it is wise also to beware of
simplisms. Too often students have heard that the God of
the Jews is only the fiery-tempered Jehovah, and the God of
the Christians is nothing more than Jesus the Warm Fuzzy.

It is undeniable that the Jews' most profound insight
into the nature of God and their relationship to God was the
covenant relationship of Sinai and the Song of Songs. Still,
one can't deny that God filtered through the sensibilities of
the Hebrews does frequently come off as more sadistic than
Ghengis Khan, demanding wholesale slaughter of popula-
tions many of whom were presumably innocent and that the
psalmists can often be both waspish and vindictive.

The Christian insights into God, embodied in Jesus,
have too often impressed on children that God is somehow a

pushover who forgives even when we have no time or inclination to apologize. It is surely true that God created us out of sheer love, before we could have done anything to deserve existence, that God loves us helplessly as a mother loves her child nine months before she's even seen him/her, that God loves us even when we sin, as a mother loves her child on death row. It is also true that when Jesus dealt with sinners in the gospels, he never once demanded that the penitent grovel or come up with species and number, and he never demanded a penance—much less "temporal punishment due to sin" even after it had ostensibly been forgiven. But the sinner does have to come home and apologize, not because God needs it but because the sinner needs it. The father of the prodigal son forgave the boy before he even left the property, but the boy had to come back for forgiveness to be activated.

3

Understanding Oneself

When I was a child, I used to talk like a child, and think
like a child, and argue like a child, but now I am a man,
all childish ways are put behind me.

—1 Corinthians 13:11

Teenagers are just emerging from near-autism. Their
self-absorption is nearly total, whether it is immersion in
their own momentous affairs or in their own uncountable
shortcomings. They rush pell-mell and blindly through the
corridors, intent as Buddhists on getting to their next class
on time, heedless that they're using their book bags as
weapons. Most have cocooned themselves from a decade of
ingesting meaningless "stuff"; at the very latest by eighth
grade most have found how to minimize the input and maxi-
mize the return; most don't read what you ask; most are
immured in certitudes they have never examined. It is as if
anyone outside the limits of their own skin—and perhaps
one or two others—is not in any genuine sense "real." And
their "love" lives are soap-operatic. One day recently, a boy
said to me privately, "I love her so much that, if I slow-
danced with her and found she wasn't mine, I'd die." I almost barfed.

But you *can't* let it get to you. Somehow you have to set a goal as a teacher far lower than you might have had when you came out of college. If your expectations are *too* high, you'll be out of teaching in a year or two, to our mutual impoverishment. My patron saint as a catechist is Annie Sullivan. How many months did she draw "meaningless" signs in Helen Keller's uncomprehending hands? In fact, Helen kept batting her away. She didn't *want* her self-absorbed darkness intruded upon. But Annie kept on, trusting. We can't teach faith unless we practice it.

Adol*escence* is inchoative. That "-escence" means a process has begun but is by no means complete, as in "conval*escence*." They may be physical grown-ups, but they're by no means psychological adults yet. Unfortunately in America most parents and teenagers act as if that weren't true. Parents think adulthood doesn't "click on" till the issuance of a college diploma when they get out of the house; teenagers think adulthood "clicks on" at puberty, when they think they're capable of handling such adult toys as sex and drinking. It's as if at age twelve they drop into a kind of moratorium, like Snow White in her crystal coffin. On the contrary, they have to be challenged, relentlessly, day after day. Any good parent with an infant has to keep on insisting that the child try to stand, to move without support, to reach just a bit further than yesterday. It ought to be no different with adolescents. Neither infancy nor adolescence is a "stage." Each is a *process.* And if we give up hope, if we lose patience, then not only are we failing at our chosen tasks, but the infant and the adolescent atrophy.

We have to take them where they *are,* and we have to move by *baby* steps—not dump *Crime and Punishment* on them, as I did as a beginning English teacher. We have to engage in *pre*-evangelization before we give them the gospel, and that will mean the class won't look very overtly "religious" for a while. But we have to till the soil before we plant the seed; like wise advertisers, we have to create the need *before* we offer the solution. At every step we have to be aware of the *psychology of conversion:* first, acknowledging that they are indeed baptized but that they have never undergone a significant conversion experience and, second, that conversion is also a gradual *process.* All we can do is hope that we edge them along a bit.

Remember my rightful deflation by the history chair. I'm just a matchmaker, trying to entice the kids to accept God and Jesus Christ. And in nearly every case, I will never know the results. There will be only a few rare (and wonderful!) letters saying, "I finally understood what you were driving at. You were right." So now I've set my goals significantly lower: if at the end of the year four or five are puzzled into thinking I might just know and have something worthwhile, then I'm satisfied. At his death, even Jesus didn't have that much.

Yet we ought not only to acknowledge teenagers' narcissism but capitalize on it. They *want* to feel good about themselves. Therefore, we have to convince them that they are in *fact* too good to demean themselves to cheat or lie, and we have to convince them that, in minimizing the input, they are selling a very good person very short. When a student consistently proves by mediocre grades that he or she simply isn't even putting in the effort to read the text, write on the top of the quiz, "Donny, don't you have any pride in yourself?"

One reaction paper asks: "Some eccentric millionaire gives you $5,000, with the only stipulation that you spend it on five different things. Which five would you *honestly* choose? Then, what do your choices tell you about yourself?" It's disheartening but enlightening, after eleven years of Christian education, to read how few would give one of those (undeserved) grands to charity. Nearly all limit the gifts to themselves, their families, their friends. I usually write in the margin (always, as on "Jeopardy," putting it in the form of a question): "Your radius of concern is pretty narrow, Ellen, no?" Many also write, "I know this may seem selfish but . . ." Write: "Aren't 'may' and 'seem' self-deceptive, Joe?" Don't give them answers. Intrigue—or irritate—them into finding their own.

That consistent response of students over the last twenty-five years supports psychologist Lawrence Kohlberg's studies of moral (human) awareness. The majority of students are at Kohlberg's Stage Three (group loyalty). But that is not only not bad but about as good as could be expected at that age. At least they've progressed from Stages One (fear) and Two (hope of personal gain), and some even seem to be reaching for Stage Four (obligation to society).

As a result of studying thousands of subjects through their responses to moral dilemmas, Kohlberg (who is not without his flaws) showed that the moral progress of an individual *can* move from the Pre-conventional (self-absorption), to the Conventional (loyalty to larger and larger groups), to the Post-conventional (no longer dependent on law but rather on personally validated principles).

Pre-conventional: Self-centered—the "Child"—Id
    Stage 1: Fear of punishment
    Stage 2: Hope of reward
Conventional: Group-centered—the "Parent"—Superego
    Stage 3: Family, gang, team
    Stage 4: Law and order; society
Post-conventional: Truth-centered—the "Adult"—Ego
    Stage 5: The common good
    Stage 6: Integrity

There is a quantum leap from the self-absorption of the

Pre-conventional level to the wider radius of sharing on the Conventional level; such people are no longer thinking primarily of themselves but of others as well. There is also a quantum leap from the generally unanalyzed conformity to group rules and customs of the Conventional level to the liberated *free and reasoned* morality of the Post-conventional level; they have gone beyond the law and live moral lives not because others demand it of them but because they demand it of themselves.

The stages, too, progress outward to wider and wider concern. Stage One, fear, is the lowest motivation for moral behavior, and there are many physical adults who know no other motive than the fear of getting caught or the presence of a cop. Unfortunately, in most schools I know, the faculty and administration unwittingly connive to keep students at this low level when, year after year at exam time, teachers are warned to be ever more vigilant proctors, rather than spending time convincing students that honesty is more important to self-esteem than winning is. The only motive such people have for attending mass, for instance, is fear of hell. When we demythologize hell, so much for mass. It is toughest to get these kids to do their service projects. The only reason such students read assigned books is the fear of failure or a hassle from their parents. Later, when they leave college and there is no test aimed at their heads, they will never read a book again.

Stage Two, hope of reward, is at least a bit of a move upward, insofar as the motive is arguably positive. Such people attend mass because it will obligate God, sort of a celestial insurance policy; it is also people at this moral level who say, "I don't go to mass because I don't get anything out of it." Students at this level can be motivated only by a *guaranteed*—and preferably quick—lollipop. They will show up for practice only when it's not inconvenient; they have attention spans about as wide as a meridian of longitude; they sleep in study halls.

Stage Three, group loyalty, broadens the scope of the person's concern from the self to others who are treated with the same sensitivity as themselves. They go to mass, even when they don't get anything out of it, because it means something to their parents for the family to be together in worship. These are the majority of my students who said they'd give part of the $5,000 to their parents, for tuition, a party, a vacation. Moving up to group loyalty is the reason extra-curriculars are so important, and any student who leaves at the final bell should get a third of his or her tuition back. What's more, their participation is a form of preevangelization. It's pitifully impoverishing how many kids are satisfied with only a few pals. Every year I ask seniors to look around and count how many in the classroom whose names they don't know, how many they've never eaten lunch with. Thus, year after year, the football team eats together, the blacks, the Orientals, the preppies—when they could so enrich one another. But if we can't get them to care about one another after being cooped up together for four years in relatively close proximity, don't expect mass to be a love-in.

Stage Four, law and order, goes beyond the clannishness of groups to a sense of a mutual relationship between the self and the entire society. You ought not to expect too many of these, especially in the lower years of high school, and sometimes this moral stance can be somewhat xenophobic: "My country, right or wrong"; the president's mere word justifies a war; if it's on the books, then it's right. But there are some who have some sense, for instance, of the mass as a unifying factor of Catholics all over the world.

Students at this level write more-fire-than-light editorials and letters to the school newspaper. They run for office (which is sometimes only Stage Two, hope of reward). But these are also the kids who will continue their service projects even after their obligated hours are completed.

Kohlberg's studies show that it is the rarest of the rare to have someone as young as a high school student frame moral choices on the level of the common good, much less the more elusive motivation of personal integrity. They just don't have the equipment and the experience yet. In fact, he says that a person at a particular stage can hardly comprehend the motivation of someone two levels above him or her. Someone at Stage Two, hope of reward, for instance, would find it irrational to call the police if there were a major disturbance. "Someone else will do it; I don't want to get involved." But our job as catechists is, pure and simple, to lure them at least one more stage upward, relying less and less on the motivations of fear and more and more on the motivation of self-esteem and growth as an adult. And it takes determination and patience on our part.

It is clear that moral growth consists in a growth in awareness of the self involved with others, in an ever widening radius of concern. It reaches out from self-absorption to involvement in small loyal groups, to a sense of involvement in the nation, and beyond that to a real if slightly more tenuous relationship with the whole human family. But again, remember the baby steps. You won't find many Nobel Peace Prize candidates in a high school classroom. On the other hand, there is little likelihood your students will even vote or write letters to the editor or volunteer to help their community if after a dozen years of Christian education, they won't even raise their hands in class, if they don't know their classmates' names, if they escape school at the earliest possible moment.

The Two Crucial Questions

Educators are easy prey to the forest-trees fallacy. For so long we have taught physics, math, history, that we think that they are the purpose of education—even though we know that students will never find any use for most of what we teach. Rather, underneath our syllabi and departments, our fundamental purpose is to cure adolescence: to keep forcing young people's radius of awareness outward.

Therefore, there are two questions every adolescent ought to face: Who am I? And where do I fit in? And there are not many classrooms in which they are asked explicitly to face those two crucial questions. Let yours be one of them.

Ordinarily, answers to the first question—"Who am I?"—are rather surface: I'm a C+ student, a jock, who's way too hairy and pimply, and whose old man can't afford to give him a car; I'm a cheerleader with a cute figure, lots of friends, and I'm an A student, but I'd never want any boy to know that." Answers to that question usually satellize around surface personality rather than on character. And yet achieving character is a much more positive—and durable—motivation for moral (human) behavior than fear of punishment, hope of reward, or even law and order.

Answers to the second question—"Where do I fit in?"—are also usually pretty surface, focusing on what job I'm going to get. Yet despite even that narrow focus, surprisingly many students don't even know what they're going to do in the latter semester of their senior year college! There seems to be little attempt to get many students to understand even their mutual responsibilities to their fellow students, much less their involvement in an even wider society. In my experience, such activities as Model Congress have appeal only to a very few of the very few Stage Fours. It would not be amiss for a teacher to have a class write letters to the editor—not of the city paper but of the school paper —about something in the school that ticks them off. Baby steps. The city paper has a better chance of getting a letter from these people if they've been published once. Nor is it possible to have your students have an awareness of the church community if they're not even aware of the academic community they've been in six hours a day for four years.

Who Am I?

There are some insights students can get into themselves by looking at what all human beings have in common before looking at the more difficult question of one's unique self. I would think that a teacher could not only take advantage of the self-absorption of the young but capitalize on it by taking at least one period a week for sessions called something like "What makes people tick?" or "What the hell are people for?" A bit of pop psychology to help young people do precisely the job adolescence imposes on them: evolving an adult self. It is a task far more meaningful to them—and perhaps objectively more meaningful—than studying the results of the Council of Trent or the supernatural effects of the sacrament of the sick. No graduate I've ever taught theology to has ever come back and said, "I remember what you said about the importance of Teilhard de Chardin." But just the other day a graduate said, "I still remember about that ol' Id, Superego, Ego."

Each of us is born *not much* more than a healthy little

animal. There is, indeed, a marked difference between a baby and a cub; the baby has the *potential* to evolve as a human being. But that potential needn't be activated. There is a whole spectrum of the meanings of "human" ranging from Saddam Hussein to Mother Teresa.

At birth, infants are about ninety-nine percent animal *Id,* concerned exclusively with their own needs: feeding, excreting, needing warmth, protection, assurance. For two years they are unconditionally loved. If they drop food or poop in their pants or wake up squalling, parents may be frazzled but (except for more and more child abusers) they can't blame the babies; infants have no choice.

But at about age two or earlier, when children begin to develop teeth and muscle control, it's time for the unpleasant (for both sides) process of weaning and potty-training to start. In the first place, the parents' patience isn't infinite, but more importantly the children *need* to begin taking control. They have to know that it's okay to bite the breadstick but not to bite the cat's tail. And so the child begins hearing two words he or she is going to hear in various forms for the rest of his or her life: "Good" and "Bad." For the child's own good, the parents have to begin "taping" on the child's mind a *Superego,* a survival manual of "do's" and "don'ts" that will serve to keep the child (more or less) from getting hurt, *until* adolescence, when the child should begin to form his or her own personally critiqued survival manual (conscience).

Adolescence ought to be the period in one's life when he or she begins evolving an *Ego,* a personally validated set of moral standards, a conscience, a self. Unfortunately, that is often a catch-as-catch-can enterprise, and in our culture there are uncountable escapes from it. But since the dawn of human history it has been inevitable that the young begin to rebel against the Superego, the moral corset parents have encased their freedom with. Again, this rebellion is most often blind and unreasoned, merely chafing at restrictions —even those which are eminently sensible. And if they resent parental restrictions, so much more the restrictions they believe arbitrarily imposed by the church. If a catechist is going to confront the second resistance, he or she has to confront the first one before that, since the first one has a far stronger meaning for the youngster.

One rule of thumb to offer them is this: If the restriction is based on *experience,* nine times out of ten the parents (and the church) are going to be right; if the restriction is based on *theory,* then you better get in there and reason it out for yourself (gather the data, etc.). When parents say "You'd better watch yourself, young lady . . ." they are basing the admonition on experience. "Every time I've seen somebody do that (and I include myself), they've been hurt." That is a simple matter of induction, exactly the same as "Every time I put out a pan of water when the thermometer says 32°, it goes stiff." But when parents tape on the Superego admonitions about welfare, homosexuals, race, etc., then the students ought to reason their way to a personal opinion based on the objective facts. However this is rare, unless the teacher patiently nurtures the process. Almost every time, when you have an argument in class, you aren't arguing with the students; you're arguing with their parents. Thus the students feel a double jeopardy: you are not only threatening "their" ideas, but you are also threatening their parents' credibility. But if the parents are objectively wrong, you do their children no service by knuckling under.

Where Do I Fit In?

Due to an enormous amount of media attention, it is clear even to the dullest students that we share a fragile biological ecology, a web of relationships with Planet Earth. They know that, if we violate that objective web of relationships, we'll sooner or later pay—no matter how inconvenient or financially unprofitable honoring the web might be. They can also be led, slowly and at times agonizingly, to see that we also share a web of moral (human) relationships with everyone else on this planet. In the same way, if we violate that objective web of relationships, we'll sooner or later pay—no matter how inconvenient or financially unprofitable honoring the web might be.

Just as one soda can tossed out the car window is trivial, so one little lie or cheating or character assassination is trivial. But if each of us exempts himself or herself from responsibility to the web of relationships, we end up with a trash-filled earth and a society in which no one can trust anyone else—which is pretty much what we have, on both counts. Our job as catechists, preparing the soil for the gospel, is to continue to widen our students' awareness of both those webs.

Like Kohlberg, Erik Erikson believes that human (moral) growth consists in cracking open the comfortable cocoons we have become accustomed to at each stage of our lives. He shows that each of these natural stages is a disequilibrium which threatens what we've long taken for granted and offers a chance for a new, larger horizon, spreading our concern further and further out into the web of moral relationships: self, spouse, family, school, community, workplace, nation, world. But, like human nature itself, each disequilibrium is an invitation, not a command. We are free to cling to the previous stage and be impoverished.

Birth is the first disequilibrium. For nine months we have lived in a literal cocoon, as close to Eden as we're ever going to get in this life. Everything is provided; we're warm, well-fed, floating serenely, without a single worry—because we can't think. Then, suddenly, we are ejected into the cold and noise, and the first birthday present is a slap on the butt. But without that disequilibrium, we'd die. Then during infancy, the parents have to do all they can to reestablish that womb-sense of trust. The child is as unconditionally cared for as he or she was in the womb.

Childhood begins about age two, when the child has naturally developed teeth and muscle control. As we saw, that is the time the parents begin using the words "Good" and "Bad," taping a Superego they hope will keep the child from getting hurt. That disruption of the status quo is both puzzling and upsetting for a child who cannot yet think, and it is a critical period in the child's growth. If the distancing from parental protection involved in weaning and potty training is too brusque, the child will end up fearful for a lifetime, anal-retentive, fearful of criticism, perfectionist. If weaning and potty training are too hesitant for fear of upsetting the child, the child will end up a lifelong whiner, demanding, pouty. Without that disequilibrium the child atrophies.

During the *play years,* the parents further distance themselves from the child, for the child's own good. Again, it is upsetting to be hauled away from the TV and thrust out into the cold with the other snotty kids, but without it the child will be dependent forever on others, unable to socialize with strangers, incapable of settling disputes without "Mommy" (or some other authority) intervening—and by that very hesitance parents usurp the child's autonomy, character, self.

School forces the child's awareness even further beyond the comfortable radius of the family and neighborhood. Probably the most painful disequilibrium in a child's early life is that awful betrayal at the kindergarten door, when the woman who has always been a Fairy Godmother suddenly metamorphoses into the Wicked Stepmother. Many students tell me they thought their mothers were actually putting them up for adoption! (Which shows that "Hansel and Gretel" tells a profound truth about growing up!) Yet without this disequilibrium, the child would not learn the skills he or she needs eventually to become an independent breadwinner—and thinker. Parents who think children get a better education at home may have a point, but they have a very limited idea of what education means. It is not simply developing skills at reading and computing; it is also developing skills for dealing with other human beings on an ever wider scale, broadening awareness of our moral ecology.

Adolescence is the atom bomb of disequilibriums. Everything one had become used to suddenly goes cockeyed. The body which has always obeyed one's wishes suddenly goes gangly, pocky, hairy. The mysterious sex organs give commands one is pretty sure shouldn't be obeyed, and a youngster often has no one—not even a parent—with the courage to be frank about them. Members of the opposite sex who have always been reassuringly repellent suddenly become very interesting.

It is at this stage—the most difficult of all—that they come to us, and their parents far too often believe that solving the disequilibrium of adolescence can be completely fobbed off onto us. (Urge your principal insistently to have classes for parents.)

Erikson insists that the purpose of the adolescent disequilibrium is to establish a personal *identity:* Ego, character, personally validated ethic. It is a time for the youngster to critique all those theoretical principles taped on the Superego by parents, to challenge certitudes. But that is disquieting, and a high school catechist should be no more upset by teenage resistance than a parent is upset by an infant's resistance to potty training, or a child's resistance to being forced out to play or being stranded at the kindergarten doorway. We have to be the hard place against which they hone their adulthood. Therefore, any teacher who accepts the ten-minute swamp gas essay or the copied lab report or the request for an extension is as well-meaningly pernicious as the parent who delays potty training or keeps the child secure indoors or takes on the task of teaching academic skills at home.

The stages for which we are preparing young people *demand* that they begin to establish a sense of identity, an Ego, while they are with us—but the demand can be refused.

Young adulthood, for which we are preparing them, offers a new disequilibrium: joining with another person in a relationship of intimacy and partnership. One major factor in the increasing number of divorces is that so many young people have balked at the challenge of their adolescence, have *not* found a personally validated self. Thus, they offer to someone else a self that neither in any genuine sense comprehends. It is a marriage of two children in grown-up bodies.

Adulthood ordinarily brings the disequilibrium of children, who are surely a challenge to a far wider radius of concern than just two people. Parenthood commits one to a twenty year stint at unselfishness, not only in struggling to give children what they need but in teaching them there are some things they don't need. (Ask any mother at the supermarket checkout.) Again, successful parenthood depends on the kind of self the person has evolved in adolescence. The parent has to be self-possessed enough to say, "I love you so much that I don't care if you hate me for this punishment, because I'd rather have you hate me for a while if it means you're not going to get hurt."

As we will see in more detail in a later chapter, another human reality both teachers and parents tend to shelter youngsters from is the inevitability of suffering. At each of these Erikson stages the child encounters *legitimate* suffering, undergoing loss of something one enjoys in order to achieve something far better. Teenagers have to learn that their resistance to change is not only natural but impoverishing. As Freud showed, we are subject to two opposite forces: *thanatos,* the death wish, pulling us back to inertia, and *eros,* the life wish, pulling us toward challenge, risk, growth.

Thanatos is the yearning to go back to the womb, to go back into the warm house and the TV, to stay home with Mommy, to keep the dependency of children but also the bodies of grown-ups. It's the urge to stay in the nice warm bed, to shoot hoops rather than do homework, to go right home rather than risk trying out for a play. It tempts us to yield to easy sex, booze, drugs. But *thanatos* is death.

Eros is the yearning for more, for wider horizons, to break away from Mommy and Daddy and achieve an adult self. It is worth the risk to work full-throttle on an essay, to try out for a team, to make the phone call and ask for a date. Of course security is nice, but security is death. *Eros* is life.

That's our job, before we ever have a chance to sell the gospel: convincing kids to risk life, when death looks far more appealing.

4

Understanding Scripture

"Do you not understand this parable? Then how will you understand any of the parables? What the sower is sowing is the word."

—Mark 4:13–14

Pause outside a math classroom sometime and try to follow the mind-withering logical progression of the problem the teacher is gradually unraveling on the board. And yet the kids seem to be following step by step; nobody goes cross-eyed with confusion. Then go into that same classroom, to those same students, and give them a quiz: "Explain: The burden of proof is borne by any individual or society sanctioning any act of intentional killing." You'll get: "This is saying that proof of abortion being intential (sic) is the actual child being carried by the mother," or "By getting rid of a fetus, killing is whats (sic) has happened (sic), so their (sic) is no question of what happens when the fetus is aborted." (I *didn't* make those up!)

On the one hand, they have certitudes stronger than Torquemada's; on the other, they can't parse the logical relationships in a not-too-complex statement. Part of the cause may be the passive illiteracy bred into them by the media, but part of the cause is also English teachers. Teachers choose English because they are personally excited by ideas, psychology, the big picture. A great many of us (including myself) are frustrated novelists and playwrights. But most of us aren't really ga-ga over footnotes, dangling participles, and making sure the quotes are outside the period. Math teachers seem to exult in that kind of painstaking detail in their discipline; math teachers don't mind leading the students by baby steps. That's *why* high school juniors can follow the intricate concatenations of a math formula, but they can't follow the logic of a paragraph. It may be why math SAT's are consistently higher than verbal SAT's.

The same "English" psychological type is attracted (or assigned) to religious education. Thus, we're too often tempted to bypass the baby steps and jump in with both big feet. Still, even the most eager of us would never think of dumping "Lear" on sophomores, yet we have no hesitation in dumping Luke on them. We act as if anyone who can read and understand a sentence (and many can't even do that) should be able to cope with the culturally conditioned terms, the Hebrew and Greek mind-set, the figurative language and mythic background of scriptural statements. That, as Fr. Raymond Brown says in the *JBC,* is to ask for a miraculous divine intervention in every single case.

To be sure, our task is to prepare our students to read the scriptures on their own, without a teacher, other than perhaps a reliable commentary. But they simply can't do trigonometry without having plowed through algebra; similarly, they can't do Matthew if they don't understand (1) the truth-bearing function of symbolic language and (2) the truth-bearing function of myth.

Insensitivity to the true function of symbol and myth is

a major cause of the pseudo-intellectual rejection of the gospels as naive, a tissue of inane fabrications. (And if you can undercut the validity of scripture, you can do all the sinning you want!) The simplism of both credulous fundamentalism and cynical scientism fastens on the symbol as if the symbol *were* the reality it only inadequately embodies. That is, of course, as palpably foolish as saying that the rose that stands for my love *is* my love, and when the rose wilts, my love has wilted.

Symbols

And yet how many young people have their incipient faith short-circuited when well-meaning (and truthful!) teachers say that Gabriel didn't really need all those feathers to fly from all the way "out there" in heaven to Nazareth? Or that our present woes were not really initially caused by a naked lady in a park who fell prey to a fast-talking snake? Obviously, the author of Genesis didn't expect his audience to take him literally, any more than Aesop, writing at about the same time, thought his audience believed foxes and donkeys really talked. All pictures of God are eminently inadequate symbols. God exists in a dimension of reality where matter has no meaning. Thus "he" has no beard, no right hand at which to sit, no genitals. God is not male. However, although God may be free of time and space, *we* are space-time conditioned, and we can deal with God only if we act *as if* he were like us. But we sometimes forget we're playing as if. When the admittedly inadequate symbol is threatened, the truth is thereby threatened. If the snake didn't talk, there goes Genesis! And original sin! And the whole damn shootin' match.

You have to catch students on this, and prove to them that religion is not the only discipline thus stymied with an attempt to "eff the ineffable." Even science (which kids think is rock solid) has to do the same. No scientist would say the whizzing pellet model of the atom is in any sense even a remote picture of a real atom. We've known that since Heisenberg won the Nobel prize, in *1932!* Heisenberg postulated that, if you could fire an electron at a barrier with two holes, the electron would be as likely to go through *both* holes at the same time! Why? Because sometimes an electron is acting like a pellet, sometimes it's acting like a wave. And that's hard-nosed science, guys!

The critical point is that *atoms* and *God* are not inadequate or unreal; only the way we *talk about* atoms and God is inadequate. The limitations are not in atoms or God but in *our* limited ability (1) to perceive and (2) to understand. Yet we get unwittingly arrogant. We think that once we've got an entity boxed in and labeled, we have it nailed down. No, no. All we can say about atoms and God—or any other entity—is: "We understand it better than we did before. But there's still plenty more to discover."

Myths

Similarly, most authorities like *Time* magazine and evening news commentators use the word "myth" only in its pejorative sense, as in, "We've finally exploded the myth that America can never lose a war." To them a myth is a person or idea existing only in the imagination, with no objective validation. Therefore, when we say unguardedly that Genesis is a myth or the resurrection is a myth, what the students *hear* is our denial of the truth of Genesis and the reality of the resurrection!

On the contrary, myth is a story that attempts to embody something *true,* but beyond literal, photographic depiction. Genesis is a myth; it was written several billion years after the events it describes in the first chapter and several hundred thousand years after the events in the second; it could hardly have been written by an eyewitness! But it attempts to embody something true: (1) Things obviously got here somehow, and (barring the placement of the celestial bodies on the fifth day) it follows the sequence of what we know now from science rather remarkably for someone writing fifteen hundred years ago. (2) Human beings are the only entities we know of that screw up, refuse to knuckle under to their programming. That latter fact is the only Christian doctrine you can prove from the daily papers. No lion ever refuses to be leonine, but we have daily evidence of human beings refusing to act humanly.

The events in the story of the prodigal son never historically happened, but the story nonetheless tells a truth. The events retailed in *The Catcher in the Rye* never happened, and yet it tells more about adolescent psychology than most adolescent psychology books I've read.

Baby Steps to Scripture

Ask any veteran teacher, and she will tell you—ruefully—that the students can't remember a year later even what you had them *memorize* the previous year. (A great many can't remember what you said yesterday.) Part of the reason is that they just "learned" it for the test, to pacify the teacher, not that they thought it important enough to remember. Therefore, do *not* assume that they know what symbol, metaphor, paradox, etc., mean from English class. They may remember that metaphor is a comparison without "like" or "as," but they don't understand that a metaphor is an end-run at the truth, even though they use metaphor every day of their lives. They don't realize that metaphor is often the *only* way one can even inadequately capture a reality like love, or death, or God.

"I feel like dirt. My chick just gave me my walking papers. She's got a brick for a heart." Any kid—or fundamentalist—knows what those words mean. But if you took them *literally,* they'd be ludicrous. Dirt has no feelings; this guy's dating a chicken apparently adept enough to hop on a typewriter and type out an eviction notice. She's apparently alive, even though her heart is made of fired clay. And yet you can *feel* far more meaning in it than, "I'm upset. My girl says we're finished. She's very unfeeling." Both statements say exactly the same thing, but the first gives an insight the second one doesn't.

Then show them that Jesus did the same thing! "It's as easy for a rich man to get into the kingdom as for a camel to get through the eye of a needle. . . . Happy are those who mourn. . . . If you want the first place, take the last place."

Unless you *decompact* a metaphor or symbol or paradox, it makes no sense. Symbolic language is trying to *force* you into puzzlement, so that you'll figure out the truth for yourself.

"You've never met Alfie? Well, Alfie's a pig." Now, Alfie doesn't have a curly tail and trotters, but there are a lot of things you can say about pigs and people that enlighten: he's ill-mannered, unshaven, makes untoward noises without caring who listens. The three-letter word "pig" does it more effectively and insightfully than all those other words together.

Similarly, "The kingdom of heaven is like a treasure found in a field." Oh, yeah? What's next? But if you decompact the metaphor, there is a chance of your being enlightened. Say you're boppin' along in your field and suddenly your toe hits something. Hm, it looks like the corner of a box. So you get down and scrape away and, lo! it *is* a box.

You creak open the lid, and inside is a thick pile of pearls, rubies, diamonds, emeralds, and gold! And it's all *yours!* I don't know about you, but if I were the victim of such a felicitous event, the first thing I'd shout is, "Holy (*beep*)!" Which means that, if you haven't considered what being Christian means, being adopted as a son or daughter of God, and shouted, "Holy (*beep*)!" you haven't even *found* the kingdom of God yet!

What are the symbols involved in the sacraments? Bread, wine, oil, fire, water, a crucifix. But without some extensive meditating on the meaning of those symbols, they remain empty. Kids can no longer even *taste* bread; it's only a vehicle for peanut butter or salami and mustard and cheese. In our culture, oil is nothing more than something to do with salads and frying. We've gotten so used to seeing crucifixes hanging around that we forget that *the* symbol embodying the meaning of Christianity is a statue of a corpse. If we claim to follow Christ, what does that mean we have to do?

Although there is a great dearth of meaningful religious symbols nowadays, compared to pre-Vatican II, there still are a great many of them, most of them sadly associated with competition and material success. A varsity jacket is only a coat, but somehow it's been made "holy" by a season of blood, sweat, and tears. Trophies are only cheap cups, but they're more than that to the owner. Grades are symbols; so is my Trans-Am, my Rolex, my boombox, my guitar, my record collection. At our school, each retreatant is given a small wooden cross on a rawhide string, and many wear them with evident pride when they return. But usually they fade in importance, along with the camaraderie that accompanied the process that made them important.

"If you want the first place, take the last place." When

we encounter paradoxes, we most often screw up our faces for a moment and then go on to something else. It's like, "What is the sound of one hand clapping?" Just today I asked a senior *AP* class, and even they couldn't figure it out: How can you be first *and* last, unless you're the only person in the race? It's quite simple after someone cracks the code for you: there are *two* races, headed 180 degrees away from one another. One race is the James Bond race: money, fame, sex, power; the other race is the Mother Teresa race: service without charge, forgiveness of debts, healing. The first is the world race, and we can see how successful its advertisers have been with our students. The second race is the kingdom race, toward what Christians at least claim to believe is real value. The question is not whether you are James Bond or Mother Teresa; the question is in which direction you are heading. Will your motives for choosing a career, for instance, be any different from the motives of the young atheist down the street? Unnerving question. But if the gospel doesn't unnerve you, you've never really heard the gospel.

Myths—symbolic stories—were the way Jesus taught. They should be the way we teach, too, but we have to show that stories are not always merely entertainments to pass the time. They have a very important, truth-bearing function. Since human life began, men and women have sat around campfires trying to understand their lives through stories. Every culture has had myths of creation and stories which try to show young people ways to pass through the stages of life with dignity and honor. A teacher of scripture *must* have some acquaintance with Bruno Bettelheim or Joseph Campbell or Mircea Eliade.

Start with a literal statement: It isn't easy to be an adolescent. Very true, but . . . yawn. So change it to a metaphor: Growing up isn't a single battle, it's a long, long siege. That expresses exactly the same *truth,* but in a more interesting way. It's only a short step to spin out that into an extended metaphor: a story.

> *Once upon a time, there was a young man named Youth who wanted very much to be a knight—manly, mature, sure of himself and his place in the world. His tutor, a wise but rather dithery old man named Merlin, described all the adventures he'd have to endure first— the Forests of Despair, the Mountains of False Delight, the Swamp of Puberty where beautiful lilies and poison- ous snakes abound. And on and on. But Youth was rest- less with those dry lectures. He wanted first-hand expe- rience, not dusty books about people who were long dead.*
>
> *So one day he set out with his squire, Hope, to rescue the damsel Perfecta, who had been locked away by the jealous witch, Time, within the dank dungeons of Castle Prudence. And the defender of the Castle was a Giant, Fear, who made up for an undeniable stupidity with a strength that could pop off bulls' heads like bot- tle caps.*
>
> *Along the way, Youth and Hope had many adven- tures, like skirmishes with packs of wolves from the Land of Doubt. But finally they came to Castle Pru- dence, and time after time the Giant, Fear, defeated Youth, and the boy retired from the fray in disgrace.*
>
> *But Hope bound up his wounds, and in the com- pany of a young man named Friend, Youth assaulted his enemy with them and defeated Fear, won the heart of the damsel, Perfecta, and they lived happily ever after.*
>
> *Or so we are given to believe.*

That little story never happened. I know. I made it up. But it is merely an expansion of the metaphor comparing youth to a series of battles, and it at least hints at a lot more details of that process. If you carried it a touch further, you'd have *Pilgrim's Progress* or "Everyman." Carry it still further and eliminate the overly obvious names, and you'd have *The Hobbit,* or "Star Wars," or "Indiana Jones": all journeys to discover the self, trying to embody the truth in an intriguing way.

Aesop's fables try to do the same thing, and Aesop is kind enough to paste his purpose in telling the story on the tail of the tale, for those who might have missed it.

> For many years the mice had been living in constant dread of their enemy, the cat. So they called a meeting to discuss the best means to deal with the situation. At last a young mouse got up. "I propose," said he, looking very satisfied with himself, "that we hang a bell around the cat's neck. Then whenever the cat approaches, we will always know of her presence, and so be able to escape." The young mouse sat down amidst tremendous applause. The suggestion was passed unanimously.
>
> But just then an old mouse, who had sat silent through the discussion, rose to his feet and said: "My friends, it takes a young mouse to think of a plan so ingenious and yet so simple. I have only one question to place to the proponents of this plan: Which one of you is actually going to *do* it?"
>
> *Application:* It is one thing to propose, it is quite another to execute.

Folktales have the same purpose. (Don't call them "fairy tales," since the term is slightly tarnished and since fairies hardly ever turn up in them anyway.) There is enough distance to them ("Long ago and far away"), so they don't intimidate children, yet the stories are all means to make young people better understand the *legitimate* suffering involved in passing from childhood to adolescence.

The sexual symbols in "Jack and the Beanstalk," for instance, are obvious once you look for them. The cow has "gone dry," meaning Jack's mother can no longer sustain him anymore. On the way to trade in the cow, he trades instead to a man who gives him seeds. When he returns home, his mother mocks his seeds (his pretensions to adult manhood) and flings them out the window. Next morning, there's this truly enormous thing climbing all the way up into the sky (the exaggerated phallic pretensions of adolescent boys). Jack climbs it, tricks the giant with his wife's help (the fairy godmother side of his own mother), and comes back with a bag of gold. (That'll show Mom he's a man.) But when the gold gives out, he goes up for a more permanent source of solvency: the hen that lays golden eggs. There's no more reason to climb the beanstalk a third time, but Jack does, this time not for need or greed but for the golden harp (his own "feminine" side; the harp which makes deeds of derring-do take on meaning). Then Jack cuts down his phallic pretensions and marries the harp, who has been an enchanted princess.

The same is true of "Snow White." The story begins when Snow White's expectant mother pricks her finger and a drop of blood falls on the white snow. It is because of bleeding that a child is born, and the two colors signify both the passion and the purity of sexuality. The stepmother shows up only *after* Snow White begins to mature; her mother is no longer as pliable as she used to be, no longer the fairy godmother, when the girl reaches for independence. And "I'm jealous of my mother" metamorphoses into "My mother's jealous of me." When she is hidden by the dwarfs, she must learn to do household tasks for them and do her part. Despite their warnings, Snow White allows the witch (stepmother) to tempt her with three gifts, which shows how close the stepmother's wiles are to Snow White's own desires: stay laces (her newfound woman's body), a comb (vanity), and an apple which is part white (love) and part red (passion). She eats of the red part and falls into a swoon, encased in a crystal coffin. (She has reached physical maturity but not psychological maturity.) Experiencing sexuality too soon, the story warns, can bring nothing good.

"Hansel and Gretel" tells a truth: sooner or later kids have to be booted from the nest so they can learn how to support themselves by their own wits. "Beauty and the Beast" tells children, who can sometimes be cruel, that anything ugly, once it is loved, becomes beautiful. "Cinderella" embodies exactly the same truth as Our Lady's "Magnificat."

If you prepare the ground *before* you plant, you have a much better chance that the seed will catch and germinate. If you prepare students for the truth-bearing purpose of stories—using stories that aren't "tainted" with the threat of limitations on their freedom ("all that religious stuff"), you will have an easier time teaching Jesus' parables. And don't *tell* them what the parable is driving at. Ask them: "What is Jesus trying to say *through* this story."

A close examination of the details of the prodigal son story, for instance, tells a great deal about God's way of dealing with sinners—and thus about the way God expects *us* to deal with sinners. First of all, it is the *father's* story; he is the only one who appears in both halves. When the son asks for "his" half of the money his father has worked for, the father blithely gives it to him, just as God gives us existence with no strings, allowing us to misuse it if we choose. When the son finally comes home, the father sees him "from far off," which shows he was out there every day looking for him. And the father runs to the boy, not vice versa. He won't let the boy get out his memorized speech. He simply throws his arms around the boy and kisses him: no demand for spe-

cies and number, no need to grovel, and instead of a penance he gives him a party! The second, pharisaic son is more
mean-spirited even than his brother. He is totally self-
absorbed and self-justifying.

In the earlier years of high school, I would tend to stay
strictly on the level of analyzing parables as stories which
try to convey a meaning about being a good human being
and Christian. Leave Revelation for graduate school! But also
kids can begin to understand that, although such Old Testament stories as Genesis and Daniel never happened, they are
trying to say something about human nature and something
about Hebrew history. Neither Genesis nor Daniel is any
more historical than "Star Wars," but both do try to get
across *truth*.

Again, start at a safe distance from the scriptures—
which they probably have heard too much about already
and think they know what scripture is all about. Start with
other creation myths; try Joseph Campbell. The myth of the
Cosmic Egg arose among the Dogon peoples of Africa and
halfway round the world in Tahiti. Like many creation
myths, it tries to resolve the sexual inequities of one half the
human race suffering menstruation and childbirth and the
other half not. The creator's purpose was that all humans be
hermaphrodites and all carry that burden. But one pair re-
belled and broke free early, so the creator destroyed the
other two and settled for an imperfect world. Early native
Americans believed the earth was like the rounded belly of a
pregnant woman, and all creatures awaited their proper
time to emerge—except for human beings, who grew restless and emerged incomplete. The Earth Diver myth in Central Europe postulated a diver sent down by God to pull up
the earth from the depths of the sea, but the Diver fell in
love with earth and refused to give it up. In the World Parents myths (like Enuma Elish), the Sky Father and Earth

Mother commingle their waters in a single entity and between them are born restless creatures who rupture the union of Sky Father and Earth Mother. Independently of the Hebrews, peoples all around the world had a common insight: the imperfection of human life was caused by rebellion on the part of the creatures. And so it is. Just read the daily papers.

Part of the problem of students' sophisticated dismissal of Genesis as merely a myth comes, as we have seen, from their ignorance of the legitimate truth-bearing function of myth. But part is also from their ignorance of evolution—which they understand about as well as they understand Genesis. Pictures in science books seem to them, without realizing, to be practically artists' drawings from life! On the contrary, all we have is a femur and a jawbone here, a pelvis and an axehead there. The rest of the assertions of prehistorians are reliable, but only educated guesses. The truth is we know pitifully little about evolution. Real archaeologists and paleontologists are far humbler than our students; they use the word "perhaps" a lot more because they know more.

It is pretty clear both to the evolutionist and to the author of Genesis that humans came only at the end of a gradual series of increasingly more sophisticated species. But neither Genesis nor evolution can produce an historically valid name for any prehistoric individual nor a biography nor a single prehistoric situation—simply because there is no documentation for such particular cases. Both of these attempts to access the prehistoric past—the scientific and the figurative—have to treat the *typical* event, the long-term trend, the movement of a whole population. Both are attempts to give some shape to facts that are never fully knowable.

Evolutionary science is not trying to discover *why* an

ape rather than a horse evolved into *homo sapiens* but how it happened, the sequence in which this metamorphosis took place. Genesis is trying to discover *why* human beings, of all the creatures on earth, are so special, so different, so perverse.

In the latter years of high school, I honestly believe it is not only possible but necessary to clarify for students the apparently difficult questions involved in the formation of the gospels, e.g., the synoptic question. They can handle trigonometry; why not L, M, and Q? Photocopy a page of Throckmorton's *Bible Parallels* and show how each of the three synoptics differs, e.g., in the segment on Jesus' arrest in the garden. Who is that mysterious disciple who leaves his sheet behind and runs away *after* they have "all" deserted Jesus—which is *only* in Mark? If Luke and Matthew had a copy of Mark, why did they exclude it? For a while, scholars believed it was Mark's "trademark," like Hitchcock's momentary appearance in each of his films. Now it is clear that Mark, unlike the other three evangelists, has the women at the tomb greeted by only *one* "young man in a white cloth," exactly the same words in Greek as at the arrest. Therefore, this young man is a symbol for Jesus' awareness of the supportive presence of God, which deserted him until the resurrection. Having done this more than a few years with juniors and seniors, I can testify that not only are they capable of handling it but that most of them, especially the brighter ones, enjoy the detective work. What's more, they begin to see the personalities of the authors revealed in their choices of what to include and what not. But most important, they see that the differences from book to book are not threats to the credibility of the books.

Another way to circumvent this very real and confusing problem is, before getting into the gospels at all, start once

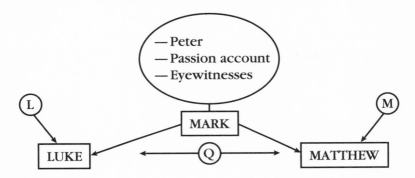

again *a longe.* Have them spend considerable time researching the life and work of some famous figure who died thirty years ago. (To placate the chair, it might be best to make it a religious figure.) They must consult not only written biographies but also find at least three living people who knew the person and write them for information. When they finish, their biographies will have been constructed exactly the same way as the evangelists did theirs. And each is, given the limitations of the writers, about as reliable as one could get.

As Mao Zedong wrote, "Do not give a hungry man a fish. Give him a fishing pole."

5

Understanding Jesus

In our own time, the last days, God has spoken to us
through his Son. . . . He is the radiant light of God's
glory and the perfect copy of his nature.

—Hebrews 1:2–3

For twenty-five of my thirty years in teaching, I have
given young people in high schools and colleges and adults
in summer workshops questionnaires. On the one hand, no
use telling them what they already know and accept; on the
other, no use playing "Onward Christian Soldiers" to con-
scientious objectors with their fingers in their ears. Two of
those questions are apropos here: What are the absolute essentials of Christianity, and what is God like?

What are the non-negotiables of Christianity: the points
of doctrine all Christians agree on, without which you cannot be legitimately called Christian—which you can deny
and still be a good person, perhaps even a saint (like Gandhi
or Camus), but not Christian? With the predictability of
sunrise, every year nearly every student writes: "To be
moral" or "To be kind to people" (usually meaning attrac-

tive people). In all those twenty-five years, I have never *once* had a student write: "To be and act like a child of God" or "To be a person for others." That's pretty ineffective "brainwashing!" How would that ethical niceness make a Christian any different from a member of the Lions Club? If being moral is equivalent to being Christian, then every moral Jew, Moslem, and atheist would be Christian.

In a related question, I ask: Will your being Christian in any way affect your choice of career, or will your motives be no different from the law-abiding atheist down the block? Again, with frightening consistency, about eighty percent answer forth-rightly that of course Christianity will have nothing whatever to do with their choice of career: "Church is church; business is business." The other twenty percent seem at first to be answering positively, but they're not: "Of course it'll make a difference. I mean I'm not gonna be a pimp or a pusher or something." In their eyes, Christianity is merely a limitation on their choices, not a challenge. After eleven years of indoctrination, they don't even know what Christianity *means.*

When I ask the second question, about what God is like, the answers are just as predictably vague: "He's some kind of . . . Force," probably influenced more by Steven Spielberg than by the scriptures. God is some kind of impersonal, mindless, and therefore undemanding eminence, who at any rate lives "way out there" somewhere and can be blissfully ignored for a long, long time. One student summed up the opinions of many very well: "I had—and I still have to some degree—the assumption that you can treat God like a wimp. Like I can do whatever I want, and God'll just forget about it, no matter how I really feel. I felt I could really mess up, but it'd be no problem. It really isn't possible to have a relationship with a wimpy God."

Jesus' Appearance and Personality

And where do they get that idea? Well, if Jesus is the embodiment of God, "the perfect copy of his nature," then they get their idea of God's personality from Jesus' personality. And where do they get their idea of Jesus' personality? Not from the scriptures, surely. They get their idea from crummy church art and even more from biblical movies, which are nearly without exception consoling lies. Even in the best, like Zefferelli's, Jesus appears hardly human, much less male: long tapering fingers, blue eyes, looking vaguely "disconnected" and ill at ease with these grubby, ill-smelling disciples, like a concert pianist slumming on the docks.

But the real flesh-and-blood Jesus simply couldn't have looked like the "man" in biblical movies. He was a Jew. Look at the skin of any Palestinian male who works outdoors all day. It's rare that he would have blue eyes. He was a carpenter for about twenty years; look at a carpenter's hands. Think of that wimpy biblical-movie Jesus scourged with leaded whips, battered around by the soldiers, booted through the streets, suffering railroad spikes through his wrists and ankles—and then taking three hours to die. Possible; unlikely.

The Jesus of cheap religious art is so unworldly he could hardly be a realistic role model; he's hardly a human being. Would anyone want to invite him home for Sunday brunch after mass? What would you *say* to him?

The Jesus of cheap religious art is not the Jesus of the scriptures; he's the Jesus we *want* him to be—flaccid, prissy, spineless, undemanding—dismissable. He's a Jesus to give guilt complexes to our rebellious Ids. But the fiery Id born in each of us is not a total enemy, as Puritans believe. In fact, to totally suppress the Id does not make it go away; it retires within and builds up steam that will sooner or later erupt in violence or pornography. The Id is like fire; unchecked, it becomes ruinous; controlled, it is a source of power, creativity, the courage not to knuckle under to vested interests. Jesus did, indeed, say, "Turn the other cheek" and "I am meek and gentle of heart." But he also said he expected to hear us from the housetops. He also consorted with whores, grafters, and other social undesirables. He also ran roughshod through a lot of "we've always done it this way" assertions. He also called the priests and prelates of his own religion "whitewashed tombs, tangle of vipers, hypocrites," among other uncomplimentary and imprudent names. In fact, in the entire gospels, I can't find a single place where Jesus bawls out a single person *except* the clergy. He also ran the temple profiteers out with nothing but a handful of rope and his own righteous indignation. To do justice to Jesus' executioners, they didn't crucify him because he was a nice moral teacher who counseled everybody to be moral and nice to one another; you don't execute an irrelevance. The people of Gadara were so afraid of what Jesus was that they "implored him to leave the neighborhood." Oh, Jesus had a finely controlled Id, all right. But that scriptural Jesus is left out of the warm-fuzzy Jesus of cheap religious art. And therefore it is left out of our students' image of Jesus.

Jesus' Doctrine

That wimpy image of Jesus—and God—has a bowdlerizing effect on Jesus' doctrine. It filters out the inescapable truth that the Christian gospel is 180 degrees in the other direction from monopoly capitalism. Consoling, but totally false. The message of Jesus is consistently *opposed* to everything we hear on media commercials ten minutes out of every hour. He kept telling us *not* to worry about what we wear, how we look, how tall we are, what we drive, how we smell. And he consistently spoke *against* the too-pervasive attitude in the church that Christians should be "sheep." "You are the light of the world! A city built on a hilltop can't be hidden. Your light must *shine* in the sight of all, so that, seeing your good works, they may give praise to our Father in heaven." Jesus didn't give us the option to be shy or reserved. Jesus was *not* always polite!

The core of Jesus' doctrine is given in the one question at the last judgment, the question which will determine whether our one life has been worth living. On the one hand, it won't be what was your bank balance or how many times did you get your name in the paper; on the other hand, it won't be how many times were you married or how many times did you masturbate. There is only *one* question: "I was hungry, I was thirsty. . . . What did you do about that?"

That is a touch too reductionist, but it will serve. Think for *yourself* what are the non-negotiables of Christianity, the doctrines without which one might be a very good person but not a follower of Jesus Christ. How does Christianity go *beyond* the morality one needs merely to be a good human being? Forget the doctrines that *divide* Christians: the virgin birth, infallibility, the real presence. What makes someone Christian, whether it's Catholic or Anglican or Lutheran Christian? I came up with four. Just four.

(1) *Jesus is the embodiment of God.* Deny that, and you can be a saint, but not a Christian. Somehow—don't ask how—the divine Word focused himself into the man Jesus Christ. If you want the definitive insight into God's personality, what God likes and doesn't like, look at Jesus.

(2) *Jesus/God died in order to rise,* so that he could uproot, once for all, our fear of death, to prove that we are not ultimately futile and meaningless. And he rose to share with us the divine aliveness, to engraft us into the life of

God. We are no longer just the human family; we are part of the Trinity family.

(3) *To become part of the Trinity family* we must give up the values of "the world" (me first!) and take on the values of "the kingdom" (them first: God and the neighbor). Our choices are based on motives 180 degrees away from the motives of monopoly capitalism. You can sum up the gospel in one word: forgiveness. Forgiveness of debts, especially when the debtor has no possible hope of expunging the indebtedness.

(4) *We celebrate our community of service at a meal.* We are a community dedicated to healing, who energize ourselves at a meal at which Jesus/God focuses himself from beyond time and space into bits of bread and a cup of wine and thence into *us.*

If you can "just" inculcate that into your students, you will have gone a long way toward making them susceptible to a gospel that, hitherto, not many of them have comprehended. Surely it's more critical that they know those basic doctrines than that they remember what went on at the Council of Ephesus or why two enormous bodies of Christians went their separate ways over the single word *"Filioque."*

Jesus' Consciousness of His Divinity

Let there be no debate over whether Jesus was only a nice moral teacher. He didn't leave us that option. On Palm Sunday the citizens of Jerusalem cheered him through the streets and proclaimed him the messianic successor to David (which isn't at all the same as being divine). The following Friday that same crowd was shrieking, "Crucify him! Crucify him!" Fans can be fickle, to be sure, but that's an astonishing about-face. The reason is that, Friday night or

Saturday morning, before the whole sanhedrin, Jesus had claimed the unthinkable. When the high priest asked, "Are you the Christ, the Son of the Blessed?" Jesus answered forthrightly, "I AM." He had used for himself the unspeakable name of Yahweh—so unspeakable that Luke and Matthew, who had copies of Mark, over-cautiously changed it to the usual circumlocution, lest they upset pious Jewish converts. But there is no doubt of it: Jesus was sentenced to death for blasphemy.

Perhaps Jesus wasn't the Son of God, but if not, then he was either a charlatan out to bilk the crowd or a lunatic deluded into thinking he was God. Yet nothing about his life suggests he was a con man; he didn't profit from his work; he didn't even have a home of his own. Nor is there anything in his message that suggests he was anything but stark raving sane. There's only one alternative.

But that leads to further difficulties. If Jesus was God, did he have the use of the divine knowledge in the womb? When Peter took him into the shop, did he just pretend he didn't know a thousand better ways to make a chair? More seriously, in the garden of Gethsemane, if Jesus had the full use of the divine knowledge, he would have known he would make it. Worst of all, at the end, when he cried out "My God, my God, why have you abandoned me?" was he just quoting a psalm to impress the crowd? Was he faking doubt and near-despair?

More profoundly even than that, if Jesus was *fully* human, he must have known doubt. That is precisely what separates us from animals on the one side and from God on the other: uncertainty. What's more, full humanity is achieved only slowly, by growing, by surmounting unexpected obstacles. It would be rankly unfair to ask humans to pattern their lives on a man who knew everything that was going to happen in his life before it happened. To accept, for example, a Jesus who was both human and not confused by sexual desires is not only impossible but an insult to the thoroughness of the incarnation. Nor will the problem be solved by some theological sleight of hand that postulates that Jesus sort of kept one intelligence separate from the other.

I believe I found at least an answer in Paul's epistle to the Philippians (2:6–10):

> *He had always the nature of God*
> *but he did not think he should try to remain equal to God*
> *Instead, of his own free will,*
> *he gave it all up*
> *and took on the nature of a servant*
> *and walked the path of obedience to death—*
> *his death on the cross.*
> *For this reason God raised him back up*
> *to the highest place above*
> *and gave him the name [I AM]*
> *that is greater than any other name.*

This does *not* claim that Jesus gave up *being* God. He just gave up the *privileges* of being God, like the divine intelligence. If it's not too clumsy an analogy, at the incarnation Jesus freely became *amnesiac* about his divinity. Thus, he learned just as we do, step by step. "He *grew* in wisdom, age, and grace."

The episode with the teachers in the temple shows that he was a very gifted boy. But it wasn't until his baptism by John that the realization came to a head: "You are the One; you are my Son." Immediately thereafter, Jesus went into the wilderness and is tempted on *precisely* that indigestible point: "If you *are* the Son of God . . ." And the temptations were real; unlike the movie-Jesus' "bulletproof" soul, Jesus must have genuinely been tempted to seduce belief with bribes, tricks, coercion. After that, his relentless attacks on the hypocrisy of the hierarchy left no doubt that there would eventually be a confrontation, and that Jesus would most likely lose. It took no supernatural insight to see that. In Gethsemane, Jesus genuinely dreaded his inevitable death; the man who doesn't dread death is not a hero but a fool. On the cross, he was tempted to the ultimate doubt, and Jesus gave the same cry as the saintly Camus: "My God, my God, why have you abandoned me?" But he clung on: "But into your hands I commend my spirit." Sheer guts and sheer faith.

This explanation of Jesus' growing *awareness* (of a divine *nature* he never surrendered) has been neither approved nor condemned by the church, but it not only resolves the problems mentioned above, but it also makes Jesus more humanly approachable. For years I suppressed a kind of resentment of Jesus' divinity: "Easy enough for him! He was God!" And I think a great many of our students harbor the same resentment, even though they may not articulate it.

Jesus' Resurrection

Everything hinges on the resurrection. As Paul says, "If Christ did not rise from the dead, then your faith is a delusion."

There were no eyewitnesses to the event—which in itself, oddly, argues for the credibility of the gospel testimony. If they were intending a cover-up, trying to make a living hawking a false prophet, think of what DeMille or Spielberg could have done with the resurrection! And many writers of the time found no qualms in pouring on the special effects.

But in the gospels there is at first only circumstantial

evidence: the empty tomb and the gravecloths. Therefore, just as we have no proof of the existence of atoms except from their *effects,* so too we can arrive at a high degree of probability of fact of the resurrection from its effects. Forget the "how." The God who could pull the universe out of nothing can do anything he darn well pleases. "There are more things in heaven and earth, Horatio, than are dreamt of in your philosophy."

Fact: Christianity apparently disappeared as an organized movement at its founder's death on Good Friday. His disciples huddled in a hideout, having completely deserted him. One of them denied even knowing who Jesus was, not once but three times. As the travelers on the road to Emmaus testified, Jesus' former followers had such hopes in Jesus, but their hopes had been shattered.

Fact: Within a *month* of Jesus' death, those *same* cowardly people were out preaching all over the place that Jesus was alive again! What's more, they continued despite beatings, imprisonment, threats from the Jewish establishment, and martyrdom. If they didn't believe Jesus was alive, why didn't they simply cave in as they had so shamefully done before?

What could explain such a 180 degree conversion? It had to be something pretty *startling* to explain such a profound change from arrant cowards to fearless apostles. The death of Jesus was a totally devastating event. Whatever triggered the turnabout had to be equally spectacular. They claim that it was the tangible reappearance of Jesus. And they went to their deaths refusing to say otherwise.

As with the minimal details of the actual resurrection event, those who testified to the risen Jesus didn't show themselves in a very good light. On the contrary, they were openly skeptical that any such event could have taken place. At first they thought it was just the silly talk of women who

had gone to embalm Jesus' body. Thomas had to put his
fingers into the wounds. The travelers to Emmaus never
dreamed that this stranger who walked with them could
possibly be Jesus, not until he broke bread with them.

However, the fact that the disciples died horrible
deaths rather than deny their belief is suasive but not
enough to compel belief in the resurrection. After all, on
November 18, 1978, nine hundred and eleven men,
women, and children willingly submitted to convulsive suicide at the order of a madman named Reverend Jim Jones.

But there is a great difference. The gospel is an open
record of what Jesus and his disciples believed. It is a calm,
life-giving, and self-sacrificial appeal, but it is an appeal not
to die for the neighbor but to *live* for him and her. What's
more, the descriptions of the escapes in Acts show that the
disciples were not running to embrace a suicidal martyrdom. And the greatest effect of all is a church which has
lasted for two thousand years, despite massive attacks from
without and disgraceful corruption from within.

There is a still further effect which fortifies belief in the
disciples' belief. They did not merely claim that Jesus was a
great prophet or even *the* messiah. They didn't even "just"
claim that he had risen from the dead. They claimed he was
God. But every single one of those witnesses was a strict
orthodox Jew, an unflinching *mono*theist. Such a conversion was even more unthinkable than from cowards to martyrs. There had to be some very convincing evidence to
bring that about. They claimed that it was the resurrection.

Those first converts weren't about to explain *how* the
Father could be God, and Jesus be God, and the Spirit be
God. (Nor will I. Nor should you.) But they believed it. To
the death. But before those deaths, they set in motion a
movement that changed the face of the earth.

So may we all.

6

Understanding Suffering

"If you want to be a follower of mine, renounce yourself and take up your cross, daily, and follow me."
                                    —Luke 9:23

A few years ago, a father came to me and said, "I'd like
to talk to you about marketing my sons to colleges." Gasp!
In the first place, he didn't even realize he was trying to
solve his sons' first genuine adult challenge *for* them. In the
second place, he didn't realize that his question was tacit
admission that his sons were inferior academic goods which
needed a little belated parental razzmatazz to mesmerize—
and dupe—college admissions officers into accepting
them. I had taught both boys, and they hadn't bestirred their
(quite modest) talents in any way, but they were "nice
kids": well-mannered, sharp looking, savvy, "popular,"
which apparently had been enough—up to the crunch
point—for their parents. Actually, they should have been
working twice as hard as their classmates, and I shouldn't
have been the only one who consistently failed them. Of
course, they graduated and were accepted into colleges. But
they got high school diplomas without getting the educa-

tion the diplomas fraudulently testified to. Their number is legion.

In *Iron John: About Men,* Robert Bly makes a strong case for the deleterious effect on any society from neutering adolescent initiation rituals to meaningless "gestures." In "less enlightened" societies, after the onset of puberty, young people are stranded in the wilderness away from their families, starved for days, subjected to ritual scarring and terrifying midnight tableaux that, almost literally, scare them into "growing up." After such an ordeal, the youngster willingly—and most often placidly—takes his or her place in the adult world, accepting both its privileges and its responsibilities.

Not so with us, either as a church or as a nation. In Christian churches, caring adults prepare the candidate *cognitively* for confirmation, but amid symbols more meaningful to experts than to ordinary children. As with Christmas, most weddings, and even many liturgies, the surface trappings have all but smothered any genuine conviction that something truly important is going on beneath them. There is little *affective* content to the confirmation/initiation ritual other than a bit of dress-up and fuss and presents, and very little internalized sense of a personal shift in the recipient's relationship to the community. The highlight occurs when the bishop gives the candidate a usually wistful tap on the cheek, and then the event is more or less quickly forgotten.

What's more, it occurs usually before the child has any genuine understanding of what the church and he or she are mutually "confirming." (Though most often, as with all religious rituals, it is not a mutual acceptance; rather, the church takes over any assertions of the will, other than submission.) Metaphors like "Now you are soldiers of Christ" might have appealed to children in a simpler age, when we felt beleaguered by all those predatory Masons, Protestants, and Jews. Now, however, the metaphor seems more than slightly corny to youngsters, especially since most of the people in the parish don't appear very aggressively apostolic. Worst of all, confirmation frequently occurs *before* puberty and certainly with no overt connection whatever with that life-shaking sexual event and (judging from the results) with no felt realization of a new, more demanding role in the community.

Outside the churches, other than the few fortunates who remain in the Scouts or young people who enter military service, there aren't even any mediocre rituals to body forth a realization not only of a new physical status in society but also (and in large part *because* of that physical change) of a new *moral* relationship to the self, to the family, to lovers, to those under whom they work, to the community at large. At least in the prosperous first world, puberty is merely an opportunity to remain a child while enjoying the advantages of an adult body.

Not that a new confirmation ritual, rigorously revamped by poets and dramatists rather than academics, would automatically usher in the brave new world or church. But the near total lack of such means to internalize a new-found adulthood and its responsibilities, coupled with a more laid-back—or even absent—style of parenting and with an even more indulgent school system, have left us with a world that is to a great extent spiritless and spineless. It is a world of children in adult bodies, wherein men and women in their forties—and later—dump spouses and families to go off to "finally find myself," a task most psychologists believe should have been at least tentatively wrapped up at the end of chronological adolescence.

The radical cause, I believe, is overly pliant parents and an embarrassingly untaxing school system, public and private.

In an article called "A Bedtime Story That's Different" (*New York Times,* April 8, 1991), Carol Lawson details interviews she conducted with parents who, however reluctantly, had learned to live with their teenage children and their dates having sex upstairs while the parents watched TV downstairs. (Understandably, they were even more reluctant to be identified.) The justifications the parents offered were painfully mealy-mouthed: at least the young people don't have to have sex in unsafe places and with people the parents don't know; better to have sex and be honest than to lie about it; "You can't tell people not to do things they are going to do anyway." Teenagers, the parents say, feel uncomfortable if they feel they're fooling their parents. The bottom line seems to be that we don't want young people to be uncomfortable about anything—despite the fact that that is precisely the purpose of adolescence: to surmount the uncomfortable, to achieve a personally validated adult self by conquering unnerving challenges.

The evidence that teenagers are avoiding those challenges—with the connivance of parents and the educational system—is both overwhelming and disheartening.

According to an Alan Guttmacher Institute survey in 1988, fifty-three percent of girls fifteen to nineteen years old had had intercourse, contrasted to thirty-six percent in 1973. That's a quantum leap in a mere fifteen years. In that age group in 1988, sixty percent of boys had had intercourse. (All of which makes the chaste minority feel left out and nerdy, but no one seems concerned about *their* discomfort.) Proposals to distribute condoms in senior high schools not only throw in the sponge on any attempt to encourage abstinence or to treat human sexual intercourse

as anything but merely a *practical* problem, but it also fortifies youngsters' convictions that more efficient birth control devices have severed any link whatever between sex
and commitment. According to the National Center for
Health Statistics, at least nineteen million unmarried young
women between fifteen and twenty-four use birth control
—which says nothing of how many young men do, and
makes one wonder if (and why) the only reason is that a
woman needs a doctor's prescription for birth control devices and a man doesn't. Despite that fact, however, there
were in one year 828,124 unwanted births and 1,368,987
abortions, and most of them to very young women—which,
in the long run, is a great deal more upsetting than being
told that sex is not just another indoor sport, that it has
inescapable human consequences.

Morality cannot be taught explicitly in public schools
because of the mind-withering belief—among otherwise
educated people—that to teach morality is somehow to
teach religion. On the contrary, one must be moral merely
to be a good human being; immorality is a rending of the
objective web of human relationships we have with everybody and everything on this planet, whether there is a God
or not. Religion adds a completely different, trans-terrestrial
dimension to those relationships. But because morality
(norms for human behavior based on *reason alone*) can't
be taught in public schools and because parents are incapable or unwilling to do it themselves or even to discomfit
their young, we are faced with a generation who are to a
terrifying extent what John McLaughlin, S.J. used to call
"moral morons."

But even in the religious schools and colleges where
I've taught, the vast majority of students routinely say sex
with one's steady or with a willing stranger is at worst a
venial sin. Class after class estimate that sixty to seventy

percent of their classmates routinely cheat on homework and exams. The majority consistently (and unblushingly) say they do not give their parents an honest day's work for an honest day's pay. There seems to be no guilt about that. Guilt, in fact, is something too upsetting to be allowed. Ditto, responsibility. Ditto, gratitude. One begins to long for an aboriginal Australian subincision ritual.

Moral behavior is not the only area in which one can discern that we dare not upset the kids. According to a 1990 survey conducted by the Institute for Social Research at the University of Michigan, U.S. senior high school students spend 30 hours weekly on school work (26.2 hours in class, 3.8 hours a week at homework) whereas Japanese senior high school students spend 60.4 hours (41.5 hours in class, 19 hours a week at homework). U.S. students spend 1.6 hours a week reading, while Japanese students spend 3.3 hours a week, and yet Japanese students watch three hours more TV a week. One major difference is that Japanese students spend less than one hour a week at sports, contrasted to seven hours for U.S. students, and the Japanese sleep seven hours less a week than American senior high students. The cult of the body may be more subtly in control of our values than we suspected.

Out of thirteen countries, U.S. students rank thirteenth in biology, eleventh in chemistry, ninth in physics; in all three subjects, only Italy is lower in scientific performance than the U.S. and Canada. One would have a far greater chance of a strong scientific education in Hungary. There seems to be a difference in national priorities, not to mention a difference in attitudes about who calls the shots in the requirements for a young person's *gradual* growth as an adult.

According to the National Assessment of Educational Progress, only forty-four percent of high school *graduates* could read at the eleventh grade level. They had difficulty in finding solutions for everyday problems: four out of five had difficulty deciphering a bus schedule; two out of three could not follow map directions; three out of four could not understand a long newspaper feature. Nearly one-third of our citizens are functionally illiterate: they can decipher street signs, but they cannot read a recipe or the helpful guidelines the government publishes for making the most out of a meager food budget. They cannot even make and adhere to a budget because they cannot add numbers.

In 1987, 26.9 percent of America's high school students dropped out. In Washington, D.C., the figure was 40.5 percent; in New York, 33.3; in California, 31.5. The effects on the job market, welfare, and street crime are both obvious and incalculable. Average SAT scores across the nation out of a possible 800-800 in 1967 were: Verbal—466, Math—492; twenty years later in 1988, they were: Verbal —428; Math—476. Our schools are not improving—and one must remember that a candidate gets 200 simply for signing his or her name. The *average* high school senior in the U.S., with a combined score of 904, is not likely to run for public office or win a Nobel Peace Prize or even vote, and roughly half of our students are *below* average. The only way to raise at least verbal scores is by reading books, beginning in kindergarten if not before, not by memorizing lists of words or taking crash courses, which is the academic equivalent of steroids. But kids don't *want* to read books; they'd rather watch a film. So give them a film.

Our purpose as parents and teachers *is* to upset the kids, to be a hard place against which they can hone their adulthood. As Dr. Lawrence Aber, an associate professor of psychology at Barnard College, says, "Parents need to set limits, and it is the children's job to push them. But when parents don't set limits, it can be scary and disruptive for children." Every parent and teacher knows what an abrasive hassle it is to face down kids with their chins set, snarling over not getting their own way. But if we don't want that job we should have remained childless or become hermits. To allow students to graduate without facing the inescapable *fact* of failure—or at least less than satisfying success—is to send them out into a minefield with no other skills than the ability to play volleyball. Too many young people have a false sense of security which leads them to believe that, at least until age twenty-two, life is going to be pretty much spring break. Or it ought to be, and anybody who tries to disrupt that is a mean-spirited Puritan meanie.

Legitimate Suffering

Most parents I know believe their job is to *reassure* their young: to shield them from harm and to provide "the best" they can for them. But to shield them from harm is to shield them from risk, from loss, from the galvanizing and soul-searing experience of surmounting suffering. If the only major setback a boy has is failure to move an inflated pig bladder through eleven other boys on a field with white stripes, if the only major challenge a girl faces is being cut from the musical, our socializing mechanisms—parents and school—not only do no long-range service to our young, but we hamstring them with a perniciously false sense of security.

If a game is worth playing, it is worth losing—and that is true both of the interpersonal family game and of the academic game as well. As Fay Vincent said, "We learn that failure often teaches us more than success. We never forget that test or paper we failed and why. A perfect grade or paper gets forgotten much more quickly. Failure is searing . . . it burns. Success is a liquid . . . it evaporates." The operative two words in that wise statement are: "and *why*."

But children *can't* fail if their overly protective parents continue to make their decisions for them, type out the envelopes for their college applications, yield to their whims (sexual and otherwise) lest the kids be upset—or, worse, dislike the parents. Our children *can't* fail—and learn by failing—if kindly (and overworked) teachers let the ten-minute swamp-gas essay slide by, if a child has gotten to senior year without the verbal and mathematical skills Hungarian children take for granted, if they *know* they can get a diploma while finessing an education. How can we hold the self-deceptive hope that our children will have spine when we refuse to display it ourselves?

Any truly caring parent should find out, with as close to conviction as possible, just what the child's capabilities are. If the counseling department offers a picture more bleak than the parent is willing to accept, there are agencies more than willing to test the child out for a fee. But after two or three reliable opinions, the parent—and the child—have to accept serenely that this is not the child of one's dreams but the child of one's love, and we will work with what we have. Settle for what the child is capable of *now*—but absolutely no *less* than that. And demand performance on that level not only of the child but of the *teachers* as well—to say nothing of the administration, which is, especially in schools depending on financial support, loath to upset parents and, *ipso facto,* to upset kids.

A youngster needs time to unwind, but many of the young I've taught in the last thirty years find it essential to keep taking breaks—to play handball, to shoot the breeze, to play the guitar, to watch TV, to talk on the phone, to go to the movies—and many of their breaks are breaks from their breaks. And when I say that, they almost inevitably grin, with a "knowing" though tolerable guilt. Get a job.

If our knowledge of young people over the past three

thousand years has not become somehow obsolete overnight, there is no youngster who is lazy—just unmotivated. There has to be a *reason*—apprehended as valid *by* the adolescent—to do this "stuff." And yet many parents and teachers are incapable of demonstrating why any sane person would submit to ingesting this "stuff." The data one will never remember, but the difference is what working on ever more complex data does to the thinking machine.

For a high school senior, five or six years down the road is a nearly limitless (and subsidized) length of time. As a result, many of the college students I deal with evenings in the dorm still can't believe, in March of their senior year, that Oz time is over; even at that late date, they don't know what they want to do with their lives. Unless students begin to internalize, at least as early as junior high, that welfare is going to come to an end in a very few years, we will continue to have a nation of children in grown-up bodies. Let them begin to pay their own tuition, to put money in the bank—not for college spending money, but for tuition. Let them begin to contribute to family vacations—not just for their own pleasures, for the family's. "If we go to Florida, you've gotta cough up two hundred bucks." After puberty, they are—objective fact—no longer babies.

Most high school students are subsidized to the tune of about fifteen grand, minimum: tuition, food, heat, insurance, clothes, car. At that cost, taking an honest day's pay without giving an honest day's work is *grand* larceny. Yet many parents blithely collude with their own children's larcenous habits.

As we have seen, Erik Erikson shows that life is a natural series of upsets, stages of disequilibrium which have a *purpose:* to crack open the individual's comfortable security and lead him or her out into a wider, richer humanity. Freud showed that it is the death wish to resent being upset, and that the life wish is willing to be upset because it sees growth as more important than security.

It is much more comfy in the womb, being pampered by Mommy and Daddy, sprawled in front of the TV, dumping school, living off the family. But comfy is the Freudian death wish, like giving candy to a diabetic or booze to an alcoholic because they whine and pout for them. With painful irony, our very attempts to shield our young and give them the best is depriving them of precisely what their puberty invites them to.

Christianity

How could anyone genuinely claim to be a Christian and yet make every effort to avoid not only suffering but even any kind of inconvenience? The crucifix, which is the symbolic distillation of what Christianity means, surely declares that it is only by surmounting suffering that we rise to new life. It is quite clear from the universe that God is "into" evolution, and it is equally clear from the natural evolution God built into the disequilibriums that invite us to keep growing. But nowhere did God write his intentions more clearly than on the cross. If Jesus is the ultimate stage of evolution that God was aiming for all along, and if Jesus "emptied himself to take on the nature of a slave, enduring death," then so must all those who claim to be Christians.

The most powerful argument against a provident God —from the tempter in the book of Job, to Voltaire's *Candide,* to "Waiting for Godot"—is the inescapable fact of suffering, and not merely the legitimate suffering that invites us to natural growth, but the seemingly meaningless suffering of the innocent we see all around us. A five year old boy once asked me, "Father, if God loves his Son so much, how could he have let him suffer so badly?'' And my only answer was: "To show us how it's done."

It's good to break students (and their parents) away from the childish notion that God is the immediate cause of all our setbacks (or even that God is there at our elbows, like a genie in a bottle, ready to leap out and satisfy our every prayer). God didn't "send" this hurricane to punish the citizens of this town; that's the same primitive kind of thinking (in the twentieth century!) that said God literally drowned the wicked Egyptians (who just wanted to be back home tending their crops). God didn't "send" AIDS as a punishment for homosexuality. *But* God did create a universe in which those things could occur. We can't let him off the hook that easily. [On this question, I would heartily recommend *Making Sense Out of Suffering* by Peter Kreeft (Servant), and I would heartily *dis*recommend the far more popular *When Bad Things Happen to Good People* by Rabbi Harold Kushner, who lets God off the hook by denying God's omnipotence.]

We are stuck with two uneasy truths: one, our belief in a purposive Mind Behind It All and, two, the inescapable fact that, in the universe that Mind chose to create, the innocent suffer. There is *only* one alternative to accepting that God has reasons to which we cannot be privy: atheism, which denies that there is *any* purpose to suffering at all. It's just your tough, blind luck that you were on the plane that crashed, that your child was born with Down's Syndrome, that you got cancer and your siblings didn't. The theist alternative is consoling, but it requires a humility few of us can muster. If Cinderella complains that she has to leave the ball, the Fairy Godmother could well say to her, "Who said you had any right to come to the ball in the first place?" There are so many wonderful events and people in our lives that resulted from our being invited into life. Who are we to complain about the accommodations?

As Pascal said, if there are only two options, one desolating and the other hopeful, and I have no way to know which is which, I might as well take the hopeful one.

The greatest obstacle to even remotely comprehending God's inscrutable will in allowing suffering is our own arrogance—and, as we have seen, the young are all too prone to believe that, if there is a reason for something, they ought to be able to comprehend it. I got a bit of an insight into that one day when I was walking along a country road, hangin' out with Jesus. A big black Labrador retriever came up with a stick in her mouth, and she shouldered me into throwing it for her. So I did, till I got tired and stopped. She came up and shouldered me again, wondering if I'd lost my sense of purpose. Just then a car came careening along the road, and I grabbed her collar and choked her back out of its way. She sniffed and snorted and walked bitchily away, looking back in anger. At that moment I was startled into an epiphany: that dog understood my motives for refusing her wishes and causing her pain about as well as I understand God's motives for denying me and jerking my chain. Humbling, but the truth.

Perhaps, then, the wrath of God *is* the love of God, assessed by a fool.

7

Understanding Morality

"Anyone who wants to save his life will lose it; anyone
who loses his life for my sake will find it."
—Matthew 16:25

Fear is the lowest motivation on the Kohlberg scale.
Although young people may generally deal with their families and friends on a higher level—perhaps Stage 3, group
loyalty—they still say they lie to their parents for fear of the
punishment. And when dealing in a wider area of relationships—school, work, the telephone company, the nation—
they say that the only norm for acting or not acting is sheerly
utilitarian: can I get away with it? What's more, that attitude
is sometimes bolstered by parents who teach them how to
play the odds and boast of cheating on their taxes. Further,
even we connive in that minimalism, offering no more motive for moral behavior than fear of sanctions if they are
caught. In every school I've served, for instance, there is a
predictable sheet from the office at exam time exhorting
proctors to ever greater vigilance, rather than spending our
time during the year giving young people motives for being
honorable. "How can you feel good about yourself, how can

you feel OK, when you routinely degrade yourself in such petty ways?"

I memorized the seven deadly sins; that didn't keep me from committing every single one of them. We played the old "how far can I go before it's mortal?" game, which the kids no longer play. In a great many cases, sin doesn't mean anything at all. Year after year, however, they do say, in response to a questionnaire on sin that we will consider in a moment, that when they do go to confession, "If it's to a priest I know, I tend to skip over serious sins," and "Sometimes I skip the bad ones because the priest says at the end, 'For these and all your sins . . .' "—and my all-time favorite: "I do pass over the big ones or twist the words around; then I confess to lying."

The reason for all this finagling around—then and now —is the same: the *reason* for the moral stricture was never *interiorized.* The *only* motivation was "The church says" or "Scripture says," never *why* the church and scripture say. It is as sheerly arbitrary as Mommy's commands to a child to bite the breadstick but not the cat's tail. That's the reason they waste so much class time trying to undermine the credibility of the church and scripture. If they can subvert the only two reasons limiting their choices, they're free! When they do something "wrong," they haven't broken a relationship between themselves and other persons (even God), but only a relationship between themselves and an impersonal "law." They are convinced the law *makes* something a sin. That is palpably foolish; it was evil for Cain to slay Abel, even though there were *no* laws, oral or written, and the ten commandments were thousands of years from publication!

To see how markedly our young people's interiorized values differ from the moral values they've been taught, photocopy the following questionnaire and give it to them. You'll be as surprised as I was the first time. No names. (I

Give your very honest opinion in each of the following cases whether the act or omission is (in most cases): [CIRCLE *ONE.*]

M = Mortal sin	V = Venial sin
S = Serious sin	N = No sin at all

a. Selling cocaine ....   M S V N
b. Buying and using marijuana ....   M S V N
c. Shooting an armed shopkeeper
    during a robbery ....   M S V N
d. Under military orders, shooting
    unarmed civilians ....   M S V N
e. Sex with a willing near-stranger ....   M S V N
f. Sex with your steady girlfriend .....   M S V N
g. Sex with another girl while going
    steady ....   M S V N
h. Sex with a male friend you honestly
    love ....   M S V N
i. Sex with a friend's mother ....   M S V N
j. Stealing $10 from your mother's
    purse ....   M S V N
k. Stealing $10 from your best friend's
    salary ....   M S V N
l. Stealing $10 from the phone
    company ....   M S V N
m. Missing Sunday mass once or twice .   M S V N
n. Getting to mass only once a month or
    so ....   M S V N
o. Going to mass only at Christmas and
    maybe Easter ....   M S V N
p. Rarely if ever going to mass ....   M S V N
q. Lying to your parents fairly
    frequently ....   M S V N
r. Lying to your close friends regularly   M S V N

s.   Lying to your steady girlfriend "now and then" .... M   S   V   N

t.   Lying to a policeman for your friend   M   S   V   N

u.   Copying a math assignment or lab report .... M   S   V   N

v.   Cheating on a final exam for 5–10 points .... M   S   V   N

w.   Having someone take the SAT's for you .... M   S   V   N

x.   Shaving points in a high school league game .... M   S   V   N

y.   Shaving points in a professional game .... M   S   V   N

z.   Inflating prices when people have no alternative .... M   S   V   N

aa. Mocking a retarded person .... M   S   V   N

bb. Mocking a "nerd" or a "geek" ..... M   S   V   N

cc. Ignoring a person you could help ... M   S   V   N

dd. Saying "F_ _ _ you" to your mother more than once .... M   S   V   N

ee. Driving while intoxicated .... M   S   V   N

ff. Habitual masturbation .... M   S   V   N

gg. Stealing from a locker consistently left open .... M   S   V   N

have given this only to boys, which may skew the evidence in my conclusions.)

Some items (e.g., sex negatively and drugs positively) show the media have done a far better job teaching values than eleven or twelve years of Catholic education. They do not think (i.e. reason to a conclusion) but rather react to stimuli. The first four questions (drugs, armed robbery, martial murder) show they can be very moral—about cases in which they have no real chance of being personally involved. They love those debates: Hiroshima, welfare cheats, euthanasia.

But things hot up when you get to the sex questions. For "sex with a willing stranger," about sixty percent say it is at worst venial; for "sex with your steady," it's about ninety percent; "for sex with another while going steady," a surprising sixty percent say it is only venial or not a sin at all. That isn't a fair indicator that all who check those are sexually active, but it does show they don't disapprove of those who do. How could they, after seeing so many TV programs? Even really good guys like Hawkeye Pierce and Sam Malone enter The Temple of Venus without a marriage certificate.

For (h) "Sex: male friend you honestly love," many circle the "Mortal" eight or ten times, and a couple usually go right through the paper—whereas all the others they had circled with only one stroke. In discussion they say such an act is unnatural, but when I respond that human sex without any commitment—just two healthy animals enjoying themselves—is also against *human* nature, they go right through the roof. Every time!

Stealing from the phone company is trivial, as are lying to a policeman or a friend or even your steady; so is copying math, cheating on a final exam. "Mass rarely, if ever" usually comes out about 50-50 serious and not-serious.

The fact that so many boys think sex with their steadies or with a willing stranger is at worst venial is more than sobering. It means our appeals to chastity and honor are quicksanded more inextricably than we thought. But in that very admission, they say that sex is not even "serious" to them. They will argue like dueling banshees that it is, but you've got the evidence right there in your hand that they themselves admit that it is not.

Kids nowadays are fortunately not as scrupulous as we were in the Cro-Magnon days when I was a kid and hell was still roaring away. But in tossing away hell, we tossed away our ace of trump, the ultimate "You're grounded!" We retired the only motivation that was going to get their attention easily, and we haven't yet come up with something to take its place. I would propose one which I find works—not with everybody, but it's a better motive than fear, and it provokes at least some students to begin taking their moral lives seriously.

Rational Morality

Earlier, I said that whenever I ask what the core of Christianity is, they almost invariably say "to be moral." The very first step is to break that false connection. And having tried it for years, I know you will not find it easy to remove; it's dyed in the wool. But it is patently false. Good Moslems, good Jews, and good atheists want to be moral; otherwise, you couldn't call them good. But being moral does not make them Christian. Therefore the two are quite separable.

The words "moral" and "Christian" are not synonyms; "moral" and "human" are synonyms. But it's tricky to show that "human" can be used in two quite different senses: "human" in the sense that one is not an animal, vegetable, or rock, and "human" in the sense of being a fully evolved human: humane, ethical, civilized.

Every one of us is born a human being, but only in the sense that we are human*izable,* whereas bunnies, bananas, and boulders are not. Cub:infant = marble:acorn. Each of the pairs looks remotely alike, but there is a vast difference. You can plant the marble and the acorn, and the marble will just sit there. But the acorn has the *potential* to become something far greater than what it started as, if it's given the proper care. Similarly, the lion cub will grow in size, but it will never become more leonine than it is, but the baby has the chance to become someone as fully humanized as Thomas More or Dorothy Day.

There is a whole spectrum in the content of that second use of the word "human," ranging from Saddam Hussein, Central Park rapists, and mob hit men to Mother Teresa. They are all human beings, but some of them are closer to merely higher level animals than others. That is, in fact, the whole purpose of a liberal education: to draw students further along that spectrum: to make them more intensely human, to make them more moral.

The Moral Ecology

Again because of the greater success of the media, even the youngest children understand that we share a fragile biological ecology, a web of relationships among all human beings on this planet and the planet itself. They know that one wrapper out the car window is trivial, but fifty thousand wrappers heap up to a trash-filled world. They understand companies that dump their toxic waste and hospital refuse mean we can't swim on the beaches. They know chemicals belched into the air have an effect on the ozone layer and will sooner or later give everybody skin cancer. They can see that you can't mock nature for too long without nature taking her revenge. That's just the way things are.

They can be led to understand that we also share a fragile moral relationship with every person on the planet, no matter how far away, a web of relationships set up by the mere fact that no one of us is more or less human than anyone else. One little lie off the lip is trivial, but fifty thousand lies means we end up living in a world where no one can trust anybody else, where we have to spend our lives in litigation because people didn't keep their promises. If you justify your cheating, then I justify mine, and don't blame me because I have the guts to cheat you in a much bigger way than you cheat me. Even if you're Little League at it, we're playing the same shoddy game. If you lie to your parents, what right have you to expect your parents to tell you the truth? Just look at the messes our cities have become because our schools are not allowed to teach morality, i.e., how to become a fully evolved human being. "It's a jungle out there," and that's almost literally true, because so many have not evolved very far from our simian cousins. If we turned their moral (human) education over to Joan Ganz Cooney and the folks at Disney, we might just have a chance.

The Porphyrean Tree

How, then, must we treat humans differently from bunnies, bananas, and boulders? We go back to the first chapter about epistemology: *they* tell *me*. No need to appeal to scripture or the church. All we have to do is *look*.

A boulder tells me what it is and how I can *legitimately* use it. It has mass, weight, electrical charge, a certain class like granite or limestone or shale. A banana has all the properties of the boulder—mass, weight, charge, class—but it can also take in nourishment and grow, reproduce itself, feed people. A bunny has all the properties of the lower classes, but it also can move around, sense danger, feel pain. A human has all those qualities but far more: we can anticipate the not-yet-real, have abstract ideas, and, most tellingly, we have conscience. As far as we know, no tiger goes into a village, steals a sheep and eats it, and then shambles back into the jungle muttering, "Oh, God! I did it *again!* I've gotta get counseling." Humans do. At least the good humans do. The bad humans don't. A clue there.

There is something *objective,* within any human being,

which makes it illegitimate to treat him or her like an animal: to harness them to plows, to herd them like cattle, to sell them like sheep. There is something *objective* within any animal that makes it unfitting to throw it alive into boiling water as if it had no feelings. There is something *objective* within any food that makes lobbing it around a cafeteria in food wars unfitting, as if it had no more ability to feed than a snowball.

Those are not based on "scripture says" or "the church says" or even on "I says." They're based on objective and unavoidable *facts*. Therefore, since humans are the only ones in that chain who *know* those facts, humans ought to *act* accordingly. Every relationship we have is a moral act because at least one part of the relationship is human: myself. Therefore, if I use a boulder as an offensive weapon, or mash a banana on someone's car window, or set a cat's tail on fire, or use someone just to get rid of my animal sexual tensions, I am not a moral person. I am acting as less than a thinking human being. I am not-OK.

There should be no need for laws forbidding people to drive crazily or torture children. The laws were written for people too dumb—or too lazy—to figure that out for themselves.

Moral Evil and Sin

Every human being is capable of moral evil: acting less than human by treating anything with less than its objective value. But strictly speaking, not every human being is capable of sin.

Moral evil is a rending of the "horizontal" web of relationships we have with all human beings and with our environment. But sin goes further; it is a rending of the "vertical" web of relationship we have with the creator who gave us all this, and set us free *not* to treat it in the way he wished —a "law" written right into the objective natures of things by their creator.

This is one of the major reasons, I think, so many kids now have no genuine sense of sin, why their moral sense comes from a relationship between themselves and an impersonal law rather than a relationship between themselves and God. You don't play "how far can I go" with a Friend. Therefore, whatever you as a teacher can do to foster that relationship in prayer, starting early, will go a long way to shore up the *natural* motivation for morality with the *supernatural* motivation of gratitude.

One of the brightest seniors I've had responded to passing over serious sins in confession: "This question explains why I think confession is kind of useless for me. I'd rather go to therapy, where I don't feel I'm being condemned, and I'd be more relaxed." It's difficult—even with bright students when they have no real relationship to God—to explain that confession is an apology to a Friend. Nor is it easy to show that, for all its evident value, psychotherapy doesn't relieve *genuine* guilt but only inappropriate guilt. Only honest confrontation and restitution will assuage guilt we feel for wrongdoing for which we are inescapably responsible. The guilt may be hushed up, but it lingers in the general feeling of "the blahs," which is the psyche trying to get the individual finally to say, "I'm *not* OK, and I've got to do something to set things right." It is difficult to show that therapy can offer plausible explanations but not the one thing humans need most: a sense of meaning and purpose.

If few of my actions can be "mortal" or "serious," then there's no reason to take me seriously.

In class after class, I find students definitely do not want to admit, "I'm *not* OK." That's a real downer. They'll admit that sixty to seventy percent routinely cheat, and yet they will not own the inescapable corollary that they are then automatically "cheats." No, I'm a good and honorable person, who cheats only when I have need and opportunity. The same is true for lying, casual sex, off-the-cuff character assassination, and failing to give their parents an honest day's work for an honest day's pay. They dig in like balky mules before an admission that—even without reference to God or to other people—any moral lapse that's swept under the rug is a lie told to and accepted by myself. A classic example of narcissism: I can preserve my "I'm OK" image, even in the face of my own genuine culpability.

"Is" ↔ "Ought"

Every "is" implies an "ought." If this thing is a watch, it ought to tell the correct time. If I am a human being, I ought to act like a human, and not brutalize, or vegetate, or use others as stepping stones. Beyond that, if someone has also been my benefactor—like God or my parents—all the more they *deserve* my respect, my truthfulness, my gratitude. If I withhold them, I am *not* OK; I am dishonorable, irresponsible, an ingrate.

But a great many of our young resist responsibility— which is equivalent to resisting adult humanity—because it is merely "a guilt trip." That dovetails with resistance to commitment; they want to keep their options open, whether in a marriage or a sexual relationship or showing up for practice. Nor do they often submit to genuine gratitude, because gratitude is one more form of indebtedness.

With painful irony, their narcissism is not rooted in over-inflated egos but in their lack of any ego at all. We all have a personality, merely from responding to the ways other people treat us. But a true ego—a personally validated ethos, the basis for claiming to have character—comes only after a great deal of reasoning and testing.

Aquinas said sinners don't think too much of themselves; they think too little of themselves. Healthy self-esteem would never demean the self to cheat on a quiz he or she will forget ever taking in a week. No one with a sense of self-worth would stoop to the quick lie, the easy lay, the "gentleman's 70"—not without soon accepting that as demeaning and making amends.

Rehabilitating Sin

Teenagers' aloofness from legitimate guilt is caused, I think, by several simplisms: the demythologizing of hell, the image of a Pussycat God, the facile economic metaphor to explain original sin, and the ludicrous division of sins into either mortal or venial. Until we short-circuit those simplisms, their cavalier attitudes will probably continue.

Losing hell as a motive seems at first a scant loss. If there were a literal hell, where have they been mining all that coal since the rise of homo sapiens—and outside time and space, too? But when we chuck admittedly inadequate symbols, we don't erase the objective reality they try to stand for: hell "says" you can't mock the natures of things and get away with it forever. Serious sin may not deliver one to sadistic demons, but real sin does have a corrosive effect on one's soul, one's self. It is quite obvious that there need be no hell for drunkards; they ingest their own punishment. But mean-spirited swine inflict less obvious but no less objectively real scars on themselves: to *be* swine—and everybody knows it but themselves.

About a quarter of each class will usually say the Pussy-cat God forgives anything, even when the sinner has neither time nor the urge to apologize. So there's no need to skid off the road to Oz on some guilt trip. I fear that image of God comes from well-meaning catechists, kindly souls, wounded by the harsh God they remember from their own youth: "God won't love you anymore. . . . Oh, that would just break God's heart. . . . God will be so angry!" Thus, they swung from God the Grouch to God the Geek—with opposite but just as tragic results: the terrifying God becomes the irrelevant God. The prodigal father of the gospel forgives even before the son has left home. But the forgiveness can't be activated until the son comes home and asks for it. If you don't think you need it, even God can't make it work.

Another knot twists in the child's idea of sin when parents or teachers explain sin with the too-easy economic metaphor: Adam and Eve committed a sin that was *so* terrible God went into an almighty snit and said we'd never be forgiven till every penny was paid back. But, since the offense was against an infinite God, there was no way we could ever pay it back, so we were all trucked off to debtors' prison till Jesus sneaked down and got crucified. Then God had to relent. But we'd still better watch our steps! That, of course, is blasphemous, but both effective and commonplace. Sin is not a debt to a Banker; sin is an insult to a Friend. But if the youngster has no personal relationship with God, a sense of that insult is not likely.

One of the worst simplisms about sin is "venial" and "mortal," as if any offense against our relationship with God were *either* inconsiderable *or* wicked enough to sever that relationship completely. Absurd but, again, commonplace. No sense of violating a friendship; no more genuine guilt than for fooling the IRS or a teacher. God is as easy to cheat as the phone company. Young people can understand an analogy to a human relationship, such as a marriage, in which there are no either/or disruptions but rather a spectrum of insults that range from the trivial *through* the ever more serious to the state where the relationship is dead. My wife's an ardent Republican and I'm a half-hearted Democrat; trivial. I flirt a bit too much at parties; that's not enough to break up the relationship, but it's not just trivial; I sleep twice with my secretary, which is quite serious but again not necessarily incurable for two spouses who genuinely love one another; I get to the point where I sleep around indiscriminately, not caring about my wife at all; then the relationship is dead—at least from my side, *even though* my wife (and God) continue loving me.

A Sane Approach to Sin

Don't mention sin till children are capable of committing it—that is, seriously insulting a genuine relationship with God. A child may do something unacceptable, but keep it between the child and parents or teacher; don't bring God in as the heavy.

Rather than stuffing heads with incomprehensible doctrines, develop a sense of the miracles of existence: birth, growth, challenge, beauty, love. God—and Mommy and Daddy—invited you into this wondrous place whose magic we must never forget or become insensitive to. God sends green life into trees, quickens the child in a mother's body, tingles under all we touch. Encourage a child to take a walk with Jesus, to talk to him, aloud even, as a secret Friend. He's there, isn't he? Perhaps that might be one of the few habits a child doesn't outgrow.

Then a child might begin to see the connection between the "horizontal" web of relationships we have with all other people and with the environment and the "vertical" relationship we have with the creator of those people and that environment in which the creator continues to in-here. Native Americans had a far deeper sense of those inter-locking webs. It is worth studying the reply of Chief Seattle to the president who wanted to buy his tribe's land: "This we know: the earth does not belong to man, man belongs to the earth. All things are connected like the blood that unites us all. Man did not weave the web of life, he is merely a strand in it. Whatever he does to the web, he does to him-self. One thing we know: our god is also your god. The earth is precious to him and to harm the earth is to heap contempt on its Creator."

Youngsters are capable of serious sin only when capa-ble of logical thinking, around puberty. They live in a nearly autistic world. Even many high school seniors have yet to grasp that all personal relationships are two-way streets, that parents have feelings and forgivable failings, too, that if it hurts when I'm mocked, it scars when I mock, that if God opened the door to wondrous existence, God deserves a public nod of gratitude once in a while.

How much better (or at least more comprehensible to a self-absorbed teenager) to see the first three command-ments less in terms of sin and more in terms of self-impover-ishment. At this stage we are dealing with young people who ought to begin moving upward on the motivational scale from self-absorbed fear and opportunism into a sense of sharing with others, and thence to a sense of loyalty.

Again, explain their relationship to God by analogy to a relationship they're more deeply aware of: Your mother carried you around for nine months, with considerable dis-comfort, risked death to birth you, washed you, sat up with you, has dinner ready for you. If that lady asks you, "Please, just forty-five minutes of mass a week?" and you refuse, you've told us who you are: a mean-spirited S.O.B. No need to talk of sin or hell—nothing but objective and unjustifi-able mean-spiritedness. We're not talking about sin, just your right to feel good about yourself. And if God opened the door to existence—the gift without which nothing you hold precious would have been possible—then God deserves your gratitude, too.

Better also to see the latter seven commandments less in terms of sin and sanction and more in terms of degrading oneself and other human beings, violating the moral web. To ignore the parents without whom one wouldn't exist, to grab another's property, to take another's only life, to use another's body as a means to self-gratification, to deprive another human being of the truth, to hanker after someone else's spouse or goods—all those degrade those people to a level below oneself, and they degrade the perpetrator, too. That's all sin is. Commandments were written for people too unwilling to figure that out.

All moral reasoning—laws, commandments, rules—is before-the-fact, warning to avoid being hurt or hurting others. *After* the fact, when the prodigal returns, the situation is quite, quite different.

When Jesus dealt with consciously guilty sinners, no one had to grovel for forgiveness, give species and number, do a penance other than trying not to sin again (no small request). But they *did* have to ask. When they do ask, Jesus says, they must receive far more than justice from a fellow Christian: open-hearted love.

The gospels are not about justice; morality is about justice. The gospels are about love. God is not our banker; God is our Father. We don't cheat our father; we don't cut corners, play games, ask how far we can go before he disinherits us. If our young are to love God—or even merely respect God—they must first meet God, person-to-Person. If we found ways to let our young meet God, they would be more likely to have a relationship with God, and less likely to insult that relationship with self-absorption. It beats fear.

8

Understanding Love

Love is patient and kind. Love is not envious or boastful.
It does not put on airs. It is not rude. It does not insist on
its own rights. It does not become angry. It is not resentful. It is not happy over injustice. It is happy only with
truth.

—1 Corinthians 13:4–7

We've all seen really ancient dollar bills. Limp and fragile as dying flower petals. The word "love" is just as frayed.
More than any other word in the language, it's overused and
mishandled—even more than the word "value." We use it
for less-than-people: "I love your diamond; I love pizza; I
love my dog." The same word we use about our mothers.
Nope. I *envy* your diamond; I *enjoy* pizza; I *care for*
my dog.

We use "love" for a bewildering spectrum of people,
too. "Love" doesn't mean quite the same thing for parents
as for siblings. Loving parents is pretty much unquestioned
and instinctive, like loving milk; loving siblings is often an
acquired taste, like loving anchovies.

And the nuances to "love" move out in ever widening
circles: the love you have for your best friend is very differ-

ent from love for your one-and-only; your affection for the pals you eat lunch with most days is different from the twist of compassion you feel seeing the enormous eyes of a starving Kurdish baby. Think of the people on "Cheers" and "M*A*S*H." The intricacies and variations of their loving one another are what bring us back week after week. And perhaps the diciest use of the word is "they're lovers." That covers the gamut from the old-shoe love of Ma and Pa Walton to the bizarre chaos of George and Martha in "Who's Afraid of Virginia Woolf?" As Yul Brynner said so many thousand times, "Is a puzzlement."

The content of the word "love" is all the more confusing for our students, who have the word bastardized almost without pause over the omnipresent Walkman. Rod Stewart had a pretty typical lyric: "I don't want to challenge you / Marry you, or remember you. / I just wanna make love to you." At best, that's a rather fast-and-loose use of words. There is a much uglier—but far truer—word to express precisely what Rod really wants. At least the Rolling Stones were honest about it. They didn't say, "I want to make love to you"; they said, "I want *it*." Especially when talking about something as mercurial as love, the first step toward wisdom is calling a thing by its right name.

Unfortunately, the resultant twists in our students' minds, about what we claim is the most important reality in human life, seem almost to defy disentanglement. They want to feel OK about themselves, but they also want to "get" as much as they can of what Rod Stewart and the Stones want, *without* paying any price. Whenever the questions arise—"Well, how far can I go, then?" and "Where do you draw the line?"—you can be sure we're not talking about love. We're talking about morality—and hardly that; we're talking about Kohlberg's first two stages: fear of getting caught and hope of personal gain.

There is *no* way two people can love one another with "no strings." Just the basic moral (human) relationship between any two human beings involves "strings," part of the moral web. And genuine love turns the "string" into a hawser. And when sex is added to the relationship, it at least ought to coat that connection with steel. That's simply the objective *nature* of human relationship, love, and sexuality. You can deny that, ignore it, act as if it weren't true. But it won't go away. And the longer you insult Mother Nature, the greater will be her revenge. Something which is meant to be one of the most beautiful experiences of human life will become commonplace.

The Spectrum of Loving

It's painfully ironic that, with students who undergo education for twelve to sixteen years or more, we rarely sit down with them and ponder just what the hell "education" means. It is just as ironic that catechists, who claim that the core of the gospel is loving, rarely sit down with them and ponder just what the hell "loving" means. As we have seen, it is a word that is incessantly used, for a bewildering array of people and objects, and we simply assume that we all mean the same things by the word. One way to begin to understand love is to see it in an ever-widening spectrum of circles of concern, reaching out at its most intense to family, to the beloved, to "the gang," to friends, to acquaintances, to strangers, to the anonymous, way out there in Siberia and Kenya and the freshman corridor. And let's not forget God.

Start with a love that no one could deny is the genuine article. The prime analogate—the model against which all uses of the word "love" should be tested—is the love of long-time spouses, who have shared miscarriages, unpayable bills, colic, midnight diapers, teething, and the whole gamut—and yet still say, "You're the only one I want to spend my life with." Genuine love is very *un*dramatic, commonplace, everyday: stirring the oatmeal love, cutting down on the drinking love, letting go of the grudge love. "I yield in this, even though I get nothing out of it, because it will make you happier."

From that we can distill the essence of genuine love. Love is *not* a feeling; it's an act of the will. Real love kicks in when the feelings *fail,* when the beloved is no longer even likable. Is that what you mean when you say, "But we really love one another"? Real love says, "I take permanent responsibility for you, even when it's inconvenient." Love is a commitment without loophole clauses. And by definition, youngsters who want to "keep their options open" aren't very good at that.

We truly do love the members of the "gang," although at least boys find that terribly difficult to entertain. They don't even like the question raised because it so (stupidly) smacks of homosexuality—which shows how completely their ideas of love are screwed up. Ask boys to think, in the quiet of their minds where no one else can go, of the boy or boys they'd really sacrifice just about anything for. Get the picture of the faces. Now, can you say, just to yourself where no one can hear you, "I *love* him"? Some can; many can't. They see the truth of it, but they just can't say it, even in the silence of their souls. But if you keep at it long enough, more will, to their enrichment.

Although the *feeling* begins to thin out as one moves out into the spectrum of circles, the affection of friends you automatically steer toward in the cafeteria is genuine love. The conversations are not worthy of etching in bronze, but beneath the chit-chat is the real conversation: "I enjoy being with you." It is sad, though, that schools at least seem to do so little about broadening that circle. At one time your best friend was a stranger, and every real friend has first to pass through that vestibule of chit-chat first. And yet in every school I've served, the blacks always sit together (right through senior year), and the orientals, the jocks, the play crowd. In class, dare them to sit at a different table, just once. You will find that even in the same class grouping they don't know everybody's name. One ploy is to pass out a class list and have each student check off the names of those in the group he or she never had lunch with. Then, when there is an opportunity to pair them up (e.g., brainstorming for an essay), pair them up with those people. It takes time, but if we can't get them even to know one another, it's unlikely they can love one another, and love is what we say we are catechists for.

Oddly, as the spectrum of concern spreads outward further from the self, and feelings thin down to near nothing, genuine love is more easily discernible—because there is no kickback to the self. Politeness and concern for the people we bump shoulders with every day, who are not even friends, just acquaintances, is genuine love: patient, kind, not envious or rude. It's a genuine gift which enriches both giver and receiver.

Concern for the anonymous who suddenly focus themselves on the news—the bereaved mother, the starving Kurdish child, the shamed convict—is very difficult to develop in the young, especially now when they are inundated in those faces well beyond satiety and the ability to provoke compassion. But if we claim to be Christians and don't try to spark such fellow-feeling, we have failed. One way is to focus students' attention on just *one* group. They can't crusade for all those in need, but they have to crusade for *something* if they are Christian. But it is important not merely to raise their compassion but also to find concrete ways to alleviate their sense of responsibility: raising funds, writing letters to the editor, contacting legislators. If we can't provoke them to stand up and be counted for even one worthy cause, Christianity doesn't have a chance.

And how do we love God, who most times seems more distant than the starving Kurdish baby whom we can at least see? The most basic way we love God is gratitude: genuinely acknowledging that we did nothing to deserve birth. Granted that if we had never existed we never would have known what we missed, but we *do* exist, and everything we hold precious depended on that invitation from nothingness. We love God by respecting his will, programmed right into the natures of things, and thus we use them as they tell us God wanted them used. We love him by worshiping with our fellow believers, often at some cost to ourselves, even though "I get nothing out of it." That's the genuine article.

How do we love God? By yielding. Letting God be God, accepting the world as he made it, humbling ourselves to accept things as they are. I don't mean Islamic enslavement to the will of Allah, which says that, if Allah made me a slave or a woman, I must surrender and be exploited. That contradicts the will of God to continuous improvement which we find manifest in evolution, in our own curiosity, in resurrection. I mean the yielding of good spouses and parents: your needs are more important than mine.

Two perniciously subtle forms of blasphemy—trying to usurp God's place—are perfectionism and its twin, the demand for certitude. Perfectionism isn't content with good enough; it's always agonizing because I didn't give 110 percent. Nope. You have only 100 percent, and that's quite good enough. Only God is perfect. Everything you do will be at least slightly imperfect; accept that; that's what loving God means. And the demand for certitude is not only blasphemous but as frustrating as perfectionism. Wanting certitude is reaching for the fruit of the Tree of Knowledge of Good and Evil, equality with God. Every answer you ever find, to whatever question, will always need fine-tuning later on. Be content with that. God made us imperfect, so we could grow.

If you consider the whole spectrum of loving—spouses, pals, friends, acquaintances, strangers, the anonymous, God—the whole essence of love distils to a single word: yielding.

Love and Freedom

Yielding is difficult for adolescents, who are scrabbling for every shred of control they can get, who in the natural order of life are and should be struggling for more and more freedom from their parents and families. There is—or at first seems to be—an objective antagonism between freedom and commitment.

Ironically, however, to be free costs. First, it costs the effort to sit down and discover just what your options are. If options exist that you don't know about, you're not free to take them, and your own inertia curtails your own freedom.

Second, you can be free *from* any outside threat or coercion and still not be free *to* act. In a college dorm, for instance, you will be free to sleep with anyone who will have you, to skip mass without Mom hollering, to get drunk for as long as your money and your liver hold out. But the big question is: Will you be free to be chaste when "everybody does it," free to go to mass when the whole dorm is snoring, free to be sober?

Third, with even further irony, your freedom doesn't start until it stops! Freedom is like money in your pocket, comforting to know it's there, but valueless until you *ex-*

pend it on what you want. You can stand in front of ten doors, perfectly free to take any one, but your freedom doesn't activate until you choose one—and thereby deny yourself, at least for now, the other nine. To be free, you have to *commit* yourself to one choice.

Finally, love itself curtails freedom. Love is a blank check you give the beloved and say, "Call that in any time —even when it's inconvenient for me." If that's not what you're talking about, you're not talking about love.

The difference between a grown-up and an adult is a matter of self-possession: taking responsibility for who one is and what one does—no excuses, no fudging, no lies. Every grown-up has a personality, but an adult has character, and "character" involves many qualities the young have always found irksome: commitment, accountability, involvement—irksome because they involve surrendering the blissful (if only apparent) freedom of childhood.

But for reasons too complex to fathom, the young nowadays are ever more wary of commitment. The *Times Mirror* research group published a survey of changes in young adults' attitudes over the last twenty years and found them "not so much disillusioned as disinterested." Respondents all over the country chose as almost a life-rule to avoid all controversy simply by ignoring its existence. In 1972, of those between eighteen and twenty-four, fifty percent voted; in 1988, only thirty-five percent voted. The only issues that engaged their concern were those that encroached on their personal freedom: drinking age, legalizing drugs, threatening recourse to abortion. This kind of spineless disengagement seems to riddle our society from top to bottom: fifty percent of new marriages end in divorce. In a recent survey, couples lined up for marriage licenses were asked if they believed this union would last "till death do us part"; sixty-three percent said no.

These are the young people who will tell you, "But it's okay for us to do it because we really love one another."

Sex

This is where you will have the biggest battles, whether it is about pre-marital sex with their steadies (about which they are very liberal) or homosexuality (about which they are more conservative—and cruel—than Torquemada).

In *Adolescent Sexuality and Sex Education,* John Gasiorowski quotes a survey of young people which asked their reaction to "I feel pre-marital sexual intercourse is immoral." In 1965, thirty-three percent of boys and seventy percent of girls agreed; in 1980, seventeen percent of boys and twenty-five percent of girls agreed. His best estimate of intercourse before eighteen: boys fifty-six percent, girls forty-three percent. If that is true, in my experience of the many juniors and seniors who come to confession in the days our school sets aside for them before Christmas and Easter, almost none trouble to mention it. But new (and veteran) teachers ought to realize when they speak about sex that, by senior year, they are talking to a group of whom roughly half believe having sex is as natural as cheating on quizzes.

One major source of that callousness toward sex is the mistaken belief that more efficient birth control devices have broken the link between sex and commitment. As we have seen before, that is patently false since, if I owe respect even to strangers, I surely ought to have a more intense respect and commitment to someone with whom I've been naked. Despite this belief, there were in one tragic year 828,124 unwanted births and 1,368,987 abortions, mostly to young unmarried women. (Abortions for rape and incest account for only one percent of abortions each year. If you add threats to the mother's life, it rises to seven percent. The rest are all matters of inconvenience.)

How does a teacher tell students they don't really understand something they themselves have actually experienced and believe they understand very, very well? Especially when, if they admit you are right, they have to give up something they like very, very much? Obviously, the principal problem is their confusion of "knowing" and "understanding." I know that dropped objects go down, but I haven't the slightest understanding why. I know my friends, but sometimes I have a devil of a time understanding why they act the way they do. I may know what sex is, I may even have had intimate, physical knowledge of it, but if I claim I actually *understand* sex—especially at age eighteen—I'm one damn fool, even if I don't realize it.

The only way to get young people to *interiorize* motives for sexual integrity is to aim your pitch precisely where your audience *is:* baptized but not converted, genial and lovable *pagans* whose choices are really based on motives no different from the atheist down the street. Such an approach does no harm whatever to the few genuine Christians; they will need a rational apologetic about sexuality when they get into those inevitable dorm discussions on the subject in a year or two.

First, again, separate morality and Christianity. We don't refrain from casual sex because we want to be Christians but because we want to be human beings and not animals. There is an objective and inescapable difference between animal sex and human sex. Both are undeniably physical encounters, but only human sex is also a *psychological* encounter, or it ought by its nature to be. If even the two partners admit that this is just two healthy young animals relieving sexual tension, they automatically have admitted that this is beneath human dignity.

Problems arise when there is, in fact, a growing psychological relationship, when the two really do love one another—but without any realistic chance of permanent commitment. In the first place, "love" is a pretty slippery label. Ask: "Have you ever really loved somebody, and then it fell apart?" At least half will usually say yes. "Then you really believed it was love, but it wasn't. How do you *know* it's love in this case, at least surely enough to justify sex?" Usually the answer will entail it "feeling different." But real love isn't a feeling; it's an act of will. In the second place, maybe religions haven't been against pre-marital sex because they were against love but because it takes something very special and makes it something commonplace. What will happen to your marriage if your spouse is "just another lay"? And religions have been around a long, long time. They've seen a lot of people get hurt.

Kids understand body language. If you're all twisted up, you "say" I'm uptight; if you fire your middle finger at me, you've "said" something, even though not a word was spoken. What does sexual intercourse "say"? (Remember: *it* tells *me*.) What does it say when two people are stark naked together? Well, you can't be any more vulnerable than that. Not just letting someone see you unclothed—and a member of the opposite sex at that—but also vulnerable in that you're trusting that he or she won't go to school on Monday and *tell* everybody how easy you are. Now *that's* vulnerable! Sexual intercourse says: "I am more vulnerable to you than I am to any of my friends, my siblings, even my own parents." Now that's vulnerable. Is that what you really *mean?* If not, your sex may be very enjoyable, but it's a lie.

Almost every time, especially with boys, someone will say, "Come *on!* If she wants it as much as you do, where's the harm?" Well, in the first place, it's pretty tough to be sure that she actually does want it. She wouldn't be the first girl to relent because she was afraid of losing the guy. In the second place and even more important, just because she wants it doesn't make it moral. If she *begged* you to make her your slave, hitch her to your plow, beat her, would that make it moral? If she begged you to help her commit suicide, would that make it moral?

The ultimate test of the truth in "But we love one another so it's okay for us to do it" is the discernment Jesus offered: "By their fruits you will know them." It's the test Paul offered his contentious Corinthians who wanted to know whether speaking in tongues came from God or the evil spirit. Does this genital expression result in two people whose joy spills over into their other relationships; does it make them more open-hearted, more generous, more understanding and forgiving? Or does it result in two people who are more underhanded, cranky, contentious?

Nifty test. And its results are as clear and incontestable as the numbers on a Geiger counter.

"Love is patient and kind. Love is not envious or boastful. It does not put on airs. It is not rude. It does not insist on its own rights. It does not become angry. It is not resentful. It is not happy over injustice. It is happy only with truth."

9

Understanding the Church

"You are Peter, and on this rock I will build my church."

—Matthew 16:18

In the minds of the young, the most fundamental question about the church is: Why bother? This is quite consistent with their natural moral development, according to Lawrence Kohlberg, hovering between Stage Two, hope of personal gain, and Stage Three, small-group loyalty: What's in it for us? Our task as catechists, then, is to try to lure them one stage further: to genuine involvement in a larger group: the parish. But too many teachers and parents set their aims far too low: merely getting them to mass. Jesus wanted more than that; he wanted us to become actively committed to a Christian community of worship and service. And the worship and the service feed one another.

Why be an active member of the church? Here is one place you most certainly *can't* say: "The church *says!*" That begs the question. The teacher has to convince quite skeptical minds that the church has a right to say anything at all. Unless you deal forthrightly with those perceptions, you

may give splendid exhortations for the young to become
pillars of the church, demonstrate the dramatic sweep of the
church's history, exegete scripture with the combined talents of Aquinas and Danny Kaye, but it will remain as academic as math, something politely endured. You are invit-
ing the Klan to join the N.A.A.C.P.

Youngsters' skepticism about the church is rooted in
four perceptions of it: the lackluster liturgy, "all those
rules," un-Christian Christians, and the church's apparent
self-antagonism.

Lacklustre Liturgy. For most Catholics, including
young people, the only place their lives and the life of the
church intersect is at Sunday mass. But only the most blindly
loyal would argue that many liturgies are genuinely celebra-
tory. For many priests, saying mass at least once every day,
the performance has become routine. There is not a single
prayer in the sacramentary geared to move the human heart;
the text was not written by poets or dramatists but by academics. The hymns sedulously avoid challenging apostles
and content themselves with telling us not to be afraid;
God'll take care of everything. Too often the musicians are
noteworthy more for their generosity than for their talent
with music or with getting a generally uptight congregation
to let loose and sing. All this, at least subconsciously, is
contrasted in the teenage mind with the full-throttle celebration of paganism at a rock concert.

There seems little any of us can do about that, but we do
not serve our students or the church by helplessly throwing
up our hands. Encourage your students to run for the teenager position on the parish council, to go (in a group!) to
the pastor and offer concrete suggestions (tactfully!) about
making the liturgy more meaningful to their particular con-
stituency. And the importunate widow in the gospel tells us
that you do not go just once. Pastors should realize that, if

teenagers are critical of the way the mass or the parish is going, they at least care enough to complain! That's a plus for our side!

If we really want to entice youngsters to become a part of the parish, the parish has to mean more to them than just a place they once went to grammar school or where they sometimes play basketball. Nor can there be any genuine sense of involvement in a group with whom they merely share the same large room an hour a week. We have to keep reminding ourselves that our primary task is to bring them more and more, every week, away from childish dependence and toward adult commitment. They have to be convinced they can make a difference.

One wonders what the effect would be on the young—and on the parish and its worship—if the parishioners combined their enormously varied skills and connections to buy and refurbish an inner-city house for a poor family: realtors, lawyers, bankers, politicians, contractors, suppliers, carpenters, decorators. Any kid can slosh a paintbrush. What a memory that would be! And for the rest of their lives they could say: "*We* did that. *My* parish." The parish might become—and feel like—a small village in the kingdom of God.

"All Those Rules." The major reason I urge teachers to teach morality from *reason* alone first is that so many who "leave" the church say part of their motive is to get away from "all those rules." When one asks what *specific* rules, they hem and haw. Some mention birth control, but according to the polls the vast majority of church-going Catholics have made peace with that. Their irritation is not with the church's rules (which don't intrude on their lives that often, other than weekly mass). It comes from confusing morality and Christianity. They think the church "makes up" the rules, that we have to be moral in order to remain Chris-

tian—rather than in order to remain decent human beings. The church enjoins few moral strictures any decent Jew or Mormon or Taoist would disagree with: honor God, parents, other human beings' rights. Our young are not resisting Christianity; they're resisting adult humanity.

Un-Christian Christians. Cocooned as they are, youngsters are unable to see the big picture; their uninformed certitudes on any subject from welfare to homosexuality are most often backed up only by one or two anecdotes: "Listen, I know this guy . . ." Thus they judge the church by what little they know of their parishes. Every catechist, within two weeks, has heard, "I know these people in my parish who are right up there every Sunday in the front, and they're the lousiest, sneakiest, worst people in the world." They also know people who haven't darkened a church door since birth and yet deserve canonization. One might well ask whether the first group might be even *worse* if they didn't come to church, and the second group might be even better if they did. (They'll bat that away because it ruins their case.)

Many students get too little of the unsung and unlikely heroes in the church today, partly because more and more are saying they have no heroes. In an *Enquiring Reporter* world, one has to be pretty flawless (and bland) to achieve admiration without some investigative reporter discovering that he or she blew grass back in college. Perhaps Catholic publishers might consider offering more short lives of people like the five Jesuit martyrs of El Salvador and the nuns who were raped and murdered there, Catholic lay people working in third world countries, VISTA, JVC. Nearly every missionary magazine has at least one such story. It shouldn't be too difficult to gather them into a single volume that would broaden the horizon of teenagers' awareness of just what the grassroots church is about.

Antagonism in the Church. This is undeniable, and like the good capitalists they are, our young realize that "when the management's confused, don't invest." The official church at least seems to many immovable, more concerned with avoiding the frustration of an ovary than the frustration of two genuinely loving and committed human beings. Frequently, on the way home from mass, youngsters hear their parents making critical comments about the pastor, his homily, his insistence on raising money. And anyone who reads the papers or news magazines realizes that theologians have been silenced or fired for views contrary to those of Rome.

This is a dicey situation which a teacher has to handle with tact. On the one hand, one has to be loyal to the church; on the other, one has to remember God gave human beings intelligence before God saw need to give us the magisterium. Mere smiling conformity from teachers on issues that divide thinking Christians completely subverts any teacher's credibility, and by that very fact subverts the validity of the rest of what the teacher offers. It's not enough to know *that* the official church takes this particular stance, but they must know *why* it does. Remember: we are not here merely to impart information; we are here to elicit acceptance.

More than that, we can no longer depend on the comforting simplism of The Church Teaching and The Church Taught; there are too many PhD's out in the pews now. The magisterium and the people of God are now like Higgins and Eliza Doolittle at the end of "Pygmalion." He had found a tatterdemalion flower girl and turned her into a lady. But once the metamorphosis had taken place, neither Higgins nor Eliza knew quite what to do about the new relationship it occasioned between them. He was no longer the know-everything teacher, and she no longer the biddable learner.

The official church not only has the obligation to listen more to the people, but the people have the intimidating obligation to speak up. And the next generation of the people of God is sitting right there in our classrooms and pews.

When a class corners me on, say, birth control or homosexuality, I consistently say, "This is the church's doctrine," and I tell them the church's doctrine. Invariably they come back with, "But what do *you* think?" And my answer is, "How do you think Jesus would handle problems of birth control or homosexuality between two people who are genuinely and permanently committed to one another?" When they persist even further, I say, "Come to me in confession, and I'll tell you what I really think." At least legally, silence bodes consent; they may guess what I think, but they don't *know*, and I never tire of telling them that. A lay teacher (or cleric) could also counter that persistence with: "I've told you what the church teaches. But, speaking only for myself, I find it difficult not to feel compassion for them."

An Organized Church

The first question to face is: Why belong to *any* organized church at all. The Catholic question comes later. There are really four reasons (at least) for belonging to a church: indebtedness, involvement, need for a director, and need for a myth.

Indebtedness. Most students have at least some vague belief that there's got to be "some kind of God." The order of the universe, the natural human hunger for permanence, the numinous hints of divine power all around us—all bolster that belief. The problem comes in the relationship which that belief automatically sets up between ourselves and such a creator.

None of us is too keen on being the subject of passive

verbs; we want to be the subjects of active verbs: "I did it all by myself; I went in there and told 'em all to go t'hell!'" But if I admit the existence of a Mind Behind It All, I *ipso facto* admit being the subject of a passive verb: I *was* created. I owe it all—everything—to Someone Else.

Whenever someone asks me "How are you doing?" I always answer, "Better than I deserve!" They're usually puzzled. But no matter how well or poorly I'm doing, I'm doing better than I have any right to demand. I didn't exist; I couldn't *deserve* anything at all. After the gift of existence, everything else is gravy. Even the crap. As Chesterton said, when Robinson Crusoe prowled the beach after his shipwreck, every tool he'd just taken for granted as commonplace before became incredibly precious. If we can make them own the fact of the gratuity of our existence and the fact of its precious finitude, the church has a chance.

Without telling them why, have students list everything in their lives they really enjoy: babies, books, beer, Bob Mooney, my mom, etc., etc., for as long as it takes. Then: "Without that gift of existence, you'd never have had any of them." Granted, if you'd never existed, you'd never have known what you missed, but you *do* exist and, my God, it's all so incredibly precious!

Also, when I admit God's existence, I admit that God is the director, not I. I may not be too keen on the part I was given or my fellow actors or the way the improvisation has been going lately, but if I go to the director and complain, he has every right to ask, "Who the hell said you could even be in the show?"

Suppose a zillionaire stops you on the street and says, "You look like a likely kid. Here's a million dollars. No strings." And off he goes. Well, if you didn't make any effort to find out who that guy was, if you didn't try to find him and say thanks, if you didn't stop around every once in a while

and tell him how you were using his gift (even if he is a bit
of a bore), you'd be a pretty mean-spirited S.O.B. Now if
God opened the door to everything. . . .

But all of us—not just teenagers—resist being be-
holden to anyone. We tend to avoid our loansharks and
pawnbrokers and bookies when we owe them. But the debt
doesn't go away. It's an objective fact. The only answer is to
accept it and live in peace with it.

Typical: "All right, I'll accept that. But why can't I just
go pray to God in the woods?" First answer: "Terrific.
When's the last time you did it?" The grimace tells you worshiping alone is just a ploy to get off the hook. Second answer: "Why either/or?" Praying alone during the week is
one of the best ways to get mass interesting again. Going to
church on Sunday and expecting to get zapped in an hour is
as silly as going on a first date and expecting to get zapped.
(Though many of the most media-addicted do expect precisely that.) What's more, like Mother's Day, having a day set
aside to worship reminds us when we get too busy that we
do need to show our gratitude. Just as we forget to show
gratitude for our mother's labor pains, we forget to show
gratitude for everything. And the words of consecration are:
"Do *this* in memory of me."

Involvement. The solitary Christian is a contradiction
in terms. Even cloistered monks and nuns are praying for the
rest of us. In the first place, part of the non-negotiable core
of Christianity is that it's apostolic; it reaches out to others.
What's more, just by the nature of human beings, we don't
learn alone, from scratch. We need the support, the challenge, the pooling of talents one can find only in a group.
We do need to affirm ourselves far more than we do, but we
also need the affirmation of others, to show us that our self-
esteem is not self-delusion. It's the way we're made. Each of
us is at the center of ever-expanding concentric circles, and

to cocoon ourselves into a tiny self-absorbed security is self-impoverishing.

What's more, I have a hunch that the number of priests and nuns leaving their offices in the church and the flow of vocations changing from a flood in the 1950s to a trickle in the 1990s is the Holy Spirit telling both "the church teaching" and "the church taught" that they have to reassess their separate acts and start some serious, challenging changes. "The church teaching" has to yield the reins more—administration of parishes, care of the "flock," and so forth, but "the church taught" has to be willing enough, confident enough, and caring enough to *take up* those reins.

Buying and refurbishing that inner-city house, together with so many others from the various strata of the parish, would give young people a felt sense of that involvement which no number of lectures could engender. The question is: Is it worth it?

Need for a Director. One year a group of upperclassmen wanted to start a lacrosse team. They had tremendous spirit but they couldn't get a faculty member to be a coach or even moderator. So they decided they'd just "get together" every afternoon and practice. Well, there were dentists' appointments. Detention. Disagreements about who'd play what and who'd come out of the game. It lasted a little less than two weeks. Life isn't like those old Mickey and Judy movies: "Let's put on a . . . *show!*" And everybody just lines up and salutes: singers, dancers, musicians, carpenters, the lot. True, a group without spirit is merely a congregation of strangers in a bus, but a group without a brain and a spine falls apart.

You can't have every player calling the plays *for the group;* we all bump into one another. In a play there are two general normative factors: the script and the director. The script usually asks the actors to stay more or less within fixed dialogue, action, and place, but the movements and intonations are left pretty much to the director and actors. Some directors are very strict (like Hitchcock) and have every move and intonation mapped out in their heads before the show is even cast. That's fine with unskilled actors, but not with pros. The best directors refuse to impoverish the combined effort by making it depend solely on *their* competence. The director may have the last word, but he or she doesn't have the last idea.

If the analogy doesn't limp too badly, the gospel and the magisterium are normative, but the church would be impoverished if scripture and magisterium were the only source of information, experience, and insight. Our job as catechists is to make children into adults who will be able to contribute to our common enterprise, and unafraid to tell the directors when they might be missing something. Loyalty to the church did not prevent Paul from standing up to the first pope, twice, and telling Peter he was dead wrong on circumcision and the dietary laws, which Peter believed were *essentials* of the Christian faith. And the first pope backed down, to the great joy of uncircumcised males and whoever in the family does the shopping and cooking.

Without mutual trust, without both discipline and freedom, many plays—and families, schools and churches—keep on going, but they fail to embody what they claim to embody.

Need for a Myth. Every society and every individual needs a myth, a freely chosen self-ideal, a map that shows us whether we're making any progress or not, which gives *meaning* to every element in the society's or the individual's life—especially the suffering and setbacks. A myth is a flexible set of guidelines for coping with difficult, unexpected decisions. But we forget that the myth of the church is an *ideal* that will never be perfectly realized. If you're working with people, that's a given. Like the North Star, the ideal church of the gospels and Acts is a guide, not a destination.

One factor in the evident malaise of modern youth which I've never seen stressed is the effect of television on their *expectations* of what life is capable of delivering. I'm speaking not just of the false ideal of external acceptability the ads portray but of the images of life it holds up and which the young subconsciously accept as "the really real." What happens in young psyches when their doctor is not as affably competent as Alan Alda, their teachers as easy-going as Howard Hesseman, their mothers as long-suffering as Jane Curtin? One wonders if the increase in teenage suicides, especially among the affluent, might be in some way occasioned by being surrounded by images of life which no human being could hope to live. The same, I think, occurs when we say in the liturgy, "Let us all thank God for the profound love we share here in this mass"—when most of us don't feel too terrific even shaking hands.

If Einstein knew what physicists discovered since his death, he'd be busting to get to a blackboard. If Beethoven were alive, I have a hunch he'd like to fine-tune the "Eroica." And if Jesus went on an inspection tour of the church today, I have more than a hunch he'd have a few suggestions. No human work or operation or theory or dogma is incapable of improvement. If you expect your self or parents or school or nation or church to be flawless, you're shopping in the wrong galaxy.

The ideal of the church is like the maps early explorers drew long before Columbus. When you contrast them to maps we have today in any ordinary Woolworth's or with actual photographs from satellites, they look ludicrously childish. But without those clumsy approximations, Columbus would never have reached the new world. Without

Galileo's now primitive calculations, we never would have been able to fling our rockets into the stars. The church is imperfect, and it's our job to make it a little less imperfect than it is today.

Why Be Catholic?

Personally, I find the church as *casta meretrix* far more appealing—in fact, endearing—than "holy mother church." What's more, admitting that the church has manifold faults also increases our credibility: "Lord, to whom else shall we go." As my former student, friend, and mentor, Wally Kuhn, loves to say, "All the boats leak. You've just got find the boat that leaks least." To my mind, for all its holes and bilge and frequent misdirections, the least leaky boat is the barque of Peter.

My best guess about why I (and most others) remain a Christian and a Roman Catholic is, basically, that I was born into a Christian, Roman Catholic family, just as I was born into its lower-middle-class values. To complain that they baptized me without my approval is as foolish as complaining that they toilet-trained me without my approval or repressed my sororicidal anger or encouraged my thrift.

When I grew up, I could critique all the "do's" and "don'ts" they taped on my superego and decide for myself which ones squared with reality and which ones didn't. That's what emergent adulthood is for. I rejected what they believed true of Jews and blacks, because it wasn't true; I accepted what they believed about anger and thrift, because it was. And I accepted what they believed about the church, far more critically than they were able to do, but basically the same church—not because they bred it into me, nor even because I had to be "loyal to my tribe." I accepted the Roman Catholic Church because I chose it.

A quite conservative colleague from a different department asked me one day, "Why the hell waste so much time teaching world religions? They don't even know the *basics!*"—a term I really didn't want him to expand on. But catechists are not only pedagogues but salespeople; we have to be confident enough in our product to *encourage* our potential customers to try out other brands. That confidence, too, increases our credibility. The customer simply has no excuse for feeling railroaded into the Catholic Church—which a great many of our students do feel.

What's more, other religions can show us not only elements of human life that we ignore to our impoverishment but also elements of our own religion that we'd never noticed were so good before. We can have our ideas of God and life enriched by anyone, by reading their books or asking them, "What do God and life look like from where you stand?"

Christian. I choose to be a Christian not only because what Jesus says makes such eminent good sense but also because non-Christian religions seem to contort the God whom I've experienced and what human life seems to be for. They express genuine truths about God and life, but they overstress them and leave them unbalanced by other genuine truths.

Immanent religions like pantheism and polytheism seem to miss the mark, at least for me; they seem to lock God—and thus our own futures—too claustrophobically within creation. And yet they do remind me, when I'm loftily theologizing about "The Uncaused First Cause," thinner than thought and colder than calculation, that I've left out of my fine doctrines the God who is "the freshness deep-down things." Transcendent religions like deism and universalism seem to err in the opposite direction, making God inexpressibly distant and uncaring, which contradicts my own experience of him. And the unchallengeable will of Allah seems to contradict the evidence of God's will to growth and evolution written in the history of the world and in natural human development. And yet Moslems remind me, when I'm in my "God's my good ol' buddy" phase, that God also dwells in unapproachable light.

Hinduism and Buddhism are so multiplex that it's difficult to box them in even inadequately. But in general they seem to me at least remotely like "The Myth of Sisyphus," life as a dreary iron round of pain and frustration, alleviated only infrequently and very temporarily by beauty, success, ecstasy, joy. Even in death there is no release but only a return to a life perhaps even worse than this one. Even those who achieve Nirvana through merciless denial of desire and self-immolating meditation seem to be preparing the self not for union with a personal God but for absorption into an impersonal All, like a bucket of water losing its identity in the sea. In a sense, many eastern religions at least seem (from my limited viewpoint) to be not only ultimately atheist but soul-suicidal. And yet the eastern religions have taught me to pray more meaningfully than any other teachers.

Catholic. I choose to be a Catholic for the same reasons: it seems like the least leaky boat in the Christian fleet. I do not believe that the Church of Rome broke away from Constantinople in 1054, nor from Martin Luther, nor from Henry VIII—though I'm no more sure (nor concerned about) whether every pope goes back in an unbroken line to the original rock than I am about how Jesus manages to get into the bread and wine. The Byzantine rites are too long for me, and like Martin Luther, "I'd rather drink blood with the Romans than wine with the Zwinglians." And yet I like Amish serenity, and Mormon generosity, and Seventh Day Adventist faith, and Jehovah's Witness courage. But they conflict, for me, with the God who made everything and saw it was good, even wine and sex and minds that could devise ways of thwarting the negative aspects of nature.

Perhaps the best way to come freely to the church is to admit indebtedness and the need for public gratitude, involvement with others, leadership, and a myth by which to map one's life. But from there on, it is not a matter of left-brain calculation, and far less of certitude. Ultimately it comes down to The Goldilocks Method: "This one is too soft. This one is too hard. This one feels just . . . *right*."

10

Understanding Praying

"I have come that you may have life, and have it more
abundantly."

—John 10:10

Praying is a bit like sex. If we engage in it, we're rather
nervous talking about it, and even the best of parents
wouldn't dream of telling their children what goes on when
they do it. In the case of prayer, that's sad, really, since
according to Jesus, we should be praying "always," and our
job as parents and catechists is to bring children and God
together.

But of course prayer is also not at all like sex, since few
of us find need for alibis about not engaging in sex: "I really
can't find the time; I know it's important, but there are so
many other things that are . . . well, you know; *laborare
est orare.*"

Not only does our reluctance to open up a few minutes
a day to God impoverish our own lives of a realization of the
genuine dimensions of those lives, but it also leaves our
young laboring as fruitlessly as Sisyphus in our theology
classes which—without a personal relationship with their

Subject—become as gratuitous and ultimately forgettable as factoring quadratics. After twelve years of Catholic education, most of our students know a great deal *about* God. But not too many of them seem to know *God.*

In class, we get so lost in explaining the signs that point to God—sacraments, scripture, rules, history, church—that we forget to make youngsters look in the direction all the signs are pointing. The God-signs become God-substitutes, to the point that children believe that if they disagree with the church, they disagree with God, and parents believe that if their children stop going to mass, they've stopped believing in God. The core reason for that, I believe, is that it is easier to teach rules and history and doctrines than it is to teach praying—just as it is easier to teach fractions and Latin grammar than to teach a love of order and a sensitivity to nuanced language. We immerse ourselves in do-able practicalities and lose the whole forest.

I trust God knew what they were doing on Mount Sinai when they gave Moses those two tablets of the law. Nice gimmick to focus the attention of an easily distracted audience. But the audience was so wedded to the tangible and to numbers that it focused all its attention on those two stone lists and forgot the light blazing from Moses' face, fresh from meeting God.

For the most part, we don't know persons analytically. And yet God (we are told in the most analytical theology classes) is personal. But our children treat him as little more than a character in a novel or a figure in history. As one senior put it: "I treat God the way I treat all my parents' friends." If God is to be known in any way other than the strictly cold and academic mode, God has to be approached as we approach any other person we want to know: person-to-Person. Till then, we're doing background research for a personal interview that never takes place.

Obstacles

The first and most difficult obstacle to encouraging the young (and not so young) to make praying part of their lives is making prayer seem worth the trouble, and the major part of this essay will devote itself to showing how *not* praying is actually self-impoverishing. That motivation does strike a chord in young people who, by the very nature of their present stage of development, are *self*-absorbed. But there are other obstacles as well: fear of silence and solitude, finding the time, the impracticability of praying and its corollary: short-circuiting the calculating intelligence.

Silence and Solitude. Probably never in history has there been a generation so addicted to noise. Put a city teenager in an Iowa cornfield and you're risking mental meltdown. I've had kids tell me that if there's no one home when they get there, they turn on the TV, the stereo, *and* the radio! What did people do when they were walking to school before they invented Walkman? But I think the reason is deeper than we might think offhandedly. My suspicion is that *their* self-chosen noise is a wall against all the *other* noise: not just screeching subway wheels and other people's blaster boxes and the shriek of sirens but against "When are you going to . . . ?" and "How come Melissa Stephenson can . . . ?" and "You guys didn't give 110 percent out there today." They're like the little boy in "My Life as a Dog": drumming his ears with his palms, shouting, "I'm not listening to what you're *say*-ing!"

Ultimately, I think, that musical fortress is merely one

more manifestation of a pervasive fear of yielding, of being vulnerable, of becoming a loser. It shows itself in refusal to admit they are wrong, even when they tell you later they knew they were. It shows itself in a refusal to commit the self—to study, to a team, to a college, to a permanent spouse, to public service, to a vocation—because something better might come along. Thus, anything teachers and parents can do to establish the context of trust also helps erode an obstacle to praying, because prayer is, after all, yielding.

Finding Time. Finding time to pray depends, of course, on the importance one attaches to praying. But those of us who will admit, however shamefacedly, "Of course praying is important but . . ." hardly ever find a day when we can't find fifteen minutes to shower, shave or put on makeup, and dress our outer selves to face the day. (Nobody's going to see the inner shambles.) Almost all of us have some kind of "fat" during the day: riding to work or school, watching mind-numbing sit-coms, talking on the phone, fooling with the guitar, listening to the stereo. Nothing wrong with them, only with a glut of them.

Impracticability. The only time praying is practical—and therefore at least remotely worth consideration—is when one is in need of a handout or some answers from God. "But God doesn't give me what I ask; God doesn't solve my problems." Personally, I've pretty much given up on prayers of petition, ever since I said mass every single day for three years that my mother could die, and she didn't. Nothing wrong with petitions; the Best of Us prayed in Gethsemane for release from the torment ahead of him. But the difference was that Jesus knew God wasn't going to answer his prayers. Like our Lady at Cana, he was simply telling a Friend there was a need. When we pour out our sorrow to a friend at a wake, we aren't expecting the friend to bring back the dead. We're drawing sustenance and strength to go on, from a friend who supports us by letting us know we're not alone. God doesn't play the game for us, just lets us know—if we allow it—that the game is played in a far larger context than we're ordinarily aware of. And I sometimes wonder if, when we pray for answers, we spend so much time prattling along about our needs that God must say, "Look, I'll *try* to suggest a few things if you'll only shut *up* and listen!"

The Analytical Intelligence. Akin to uprooting that need to dominate God is the difficulty of short-circuiting the discursive intelligence that is in full gear most of the day. Even students who don't slog away at the books nonetheless spend a great deal of time trying to outwit the rules. We add budget figures, diagnose illnesses, follow recipes, try to figure out our kids, keep to schedules—all day long, clickety-clickety-click. Somehow we've got to pull ourselves off to the side of the road and find out where the hell we're going—and why. We have to open the spirits within ourselves (which the analytical intelligence can't even comprehend), and allow the Spirit of God to invade us. But that's difficult, again, because it means yielding center stage in our concerns to the One who has been center stage since before we even joined the cast.

It is very important—perhaps critical—that parents and teachers of religion in early grade school create within the young a felt sense of the numinous all around them in nature and art and people *before* the self-absorption and defensiveness and fear of yielding arise in adolescence. What's more, I believe that is the time to begin teaching children methods of centering prayer, before the pseudo-sophistation sets in.

Push back the desks (or take them to a church) and tell them beforehand all that you're going to do before you do it.

When you finish setting everything up, you are going to leave, and any one of them may leave, too, *as long as* they are extra careful not to disturb those who want to stay. Loosen the ties; take off your shoes if you want. Now sit on the floor with your backs against something, close your eyes, and just relax. For fifteen minutes or so, the world can get along without you. Rotate your head around your neck, and let all the tension drain down into your shoulders. Feel gravity pulling all the uptightness and the control out of your shoulders, down your back, through your seat and your legs and into the floor. Peace . . . peace.

Now take a deep breath—a really deep breath; hold it for five counts; out for five counts; in for five counts; out for five counts. Think of all the air in this room; we use it, then pass it on, never knowing whom it has kept alive before us; we share that alive-giving force. In. Out. Now go beyond this room to the envelope of air that surrounds the whole earth; you're a part of that—leaving us, crossing the Atlantic and Asia and the Pacific and back to us. In. Out. Now, as you breathe in that air, say inside the innermost room of yourself: "God, my good friend . . ." and, as you breathe out, ". . . somehow you're alive in me." Say that again, several times, and quietly withdraw.

It won't work for all of them, at least the first time, but it will work for some, and "some" is more than Jesus had with him on Calvary. The important thing is to elicit their receptivity to the *process.* Before beginning, be sure to tell them not to ask themselves "What's this supposed to be doing to me?" or "Is everybody looking at me?" or "Am I doing this right?" Just yield; let go. Let God manipulate your soul. And, personally, I'm dead against some kind of prayer journal, measuring progress or treasuring "lights." That's too much like weightlifting in front of a mirror. The focus is in the wrong place.

Finally, there is the primary obstacle, for young people or for adults: What's in it for me? And that's a perfectly reasonable question. We can teach and test theology, but we can only try to convince them of the value of belief and religion. We are not just teachers; we are also salespeople.

What's in It for Me: Humanizing

A great many executives pay big bucks for weekly courses in meditation, with no overtly religious concern at all. What they want to do is focus themselves, get in touch with who they are and what is really important in their lives, see the garbage for what it is and reject it. There are many worthwhile effects from taking time to meditate which have no necessary connection with religion at all and, since grace builds on nature, perhaps we can lure them into genuine praying by showing its personal advantages to them first. Here are only five: simplification, perspective, freedom, feeding the soul, and wisdom.

Simplification. There is no emergent adult who won't admit that life is too confusing, especially today. We live in the most complex time in history: hurry, bustle, keep it moving, have it on my desk by yesterday. In every free moment our senses are assaulted by billboards and ads and commercials shouting at us to buy this, buy that—or else! There's a hydra of conflicting expectations: parents, peers, teachers, teammates, girls, boys, muggers. Report cards, college boards, traffic cops, tryouts. Who's playing quarterback and who's the prom queen? "Drop out! . . . Get involved! . . . Smoke grass! . . . Go to mass! . . . Demand your rights! . . . Do what you're told!" It's like being locked in an asylum for insane carnival pitchmen—and yet we've gotten so used to it that we rarely realize how numb we've become.

"Leave me *alone!*" Okay. Here's your chance.

Each of us, at the very depths of ourselves, has a human need to become a hermit for at least fifteen minutes a day. Not a hermit cocooned in the Walkman or music. A hermit. Unless there is an eye of peace in the hurricane of our days, we're going to be swallowed up by the crapstorm. Whenever mothers come to confession, their penance is always: "A half-hour before the kids come home, kick off your shoes, relax, and find out what's really important." No mother has ever objected.

Only for a few moments, detach yourself from everything that fluctuates and, at rest, let all the tension drain out: all the confusion, all the deadlines, all the questions. Retreat from bustle and obligations, and merely *be* there: open, emptied, at peace, receptive. As Chesterton said, poets and contemplatives don't go mad; the "solvers" do. Life is an infinite sea, but the solvers try to cross the infinite sea, thus making it finite. And all they find is frustration. The poet and contemplative float easily on the infinite sea and enjoy the view. They find peace and perspective.

Perspective. After seeing enough pictures of starving children in Kurdestan, Ethiopia, Cambodia, at least the sensitive soul feels a twinge of guilt complaining that Mom has forced tuna casserole and broccoli on us again. Similarly, pulling out of the hurlyburly for a while shows us what is really important in our lives, in others' expectations, in all those shouting voices.

One day my friend Ed Bartley was grading "Macbeth" tests at his desk when his little daughter came up and said, "Daddy! Come quick! The birds!" But Ed was a man who got papers back the next day. With hardly a look, he said, "Not now, honey. Daddy's busy." He went on, unaware for a few moments that she was standing next to his desk, a fat tear running down her cheek. In that moment, he really saw her. She was more important than "Macbeth" and "promises to keep." Wisely he let her lead him to the apartment window, and for ten minutes they looked at the birds on the roof. They weren't accomplishing anything, but something was happening. And three years later, Ed died.

William Carlos Williams says the same wise thing:

> so much depends
> upon
>
> a red wheel
> barrow
>
> glazed with rain
> water
>
> beside the white
> chickens

Freedom. The young—and not so young—almost all have a ludicrous idea that somewhere "out there" totally unencumbered freedom is possible. Even Genghis Khan was *subject* to the law of gravity. He had to submit, humbly as a child, before storms and earthquakes. Whether he wanted to or not, he had to eat and sleep, have toothaches, get weary. There was a limit to what he could drink before passing out. He was locked in this time and this self. If he had conquered all the world, he was still as powerless as a peasant before death.

But most of the limitations on our freedom are *self-*imposed: enslavement to the judgments of others, gigantification of our shortcomings, and at the root: fear. If we could just lay hold and take possession of our inner selves—in peace, beyond the power of others to warp that self-possession—we might find "the serenity to accept the things that can't be changed, the courage to change the things that can be changed, and the wisdom to know the difference."

True freedom comes from what St. Ignatius Loyola called "detachment" or "indifference." Neither term implies that a person must become insensitive. The real meaning is "impartiality," that one seeks the freedom to do the truth, no matter what choosing the best option might cost. One chooses without possessiveness, without self-serving ambition, without impulsiveness, without greed. It counts the cost to the self later—if at all.

No one can achieve real freedom until he or she can find what real freedom truly means. And one won't find freedom in living random lives.

Feeding the Soul. We are all smothered by reminders to build up our bodies—nutrition, workouts, rejecting drugs, and the young hear them with sometimes Buddhist attention. They are also smothered with reminders to build up their minds—reading, learning to think by learning to write, getting those verbal and math scores up, which the young hear with somewhat less attention. But there seem to be far fewer reminders that the one thing that differentiates us from animals is not our bodies or our brains, which they share, but our souls, which they do not.

It is not that difficult to show young people that the human soul does in fact exist, and that starving the soul is impoverishing the self, because the soul *is* the self: who-I-am. When they look at me, they don't see *me;* they see only my body. They can make educated guesses from what I say and do what kind of self I am, but they don't see that self. The guards in Nazi extermination camps had bodies and brains, but the reason we can call them "bestial" is that they had lost their souls. When I honestly fall in love, it's not the yearnings of my flesh or the calculations of the brain that say, "Yep! This is the one!" It's my soul. When I stand in awe of a snow-capped peak at dawn or Michelangelo's David or a baby's fist around my finger, it's not my body or mind that says, "Gasp!" It's my soul. My intellect is intrigued; my soul is stirred. It's where all that's nebulous in me resides: honor, awe, loyalty, remorse, patriotism, faith, hope, and love. Oh, the soul is there, all right.

The body gurgles for food, the mind itches for answers, and the hunger of the spirit expresses itself in restlessness and discontent. So, if you're suffering from The Blahs or Nothing Makes Any Sense or One-Damn-Thing-After-Another, you quite likely suffer from soul malnutrition. The hungers of the body can be temporarily assuaged by cheese puffs and soft drinks; the hungers of the mind can be distracted by ballscores and gossip; and the hungers of the soul can be silenced by puppy love and soap operas. But the result of bad food and lack of exercise are the same for all three: flab. What you need is to exercise the one thing that separates us from beasts: the soul.

Wisdom. Even kids can understand the difference between knowledge and wisdom, between someone who's a "brain" and someone to whom to bring their pain. Someone wise does know which things cannot be changed and which can, and he or she is at peace with that. The wise person accepts the true perspective of things, his or her position in the universe: far better than a rock or carrot or pig; far less than God. Science is not God, nor is Progress, nor is Money, nor, most certainly, am I.

Wisdom does not come from suffering. If it did, animals in experimental laboratories would be wiser than all of us. Wisdom comes from suffering reflected on, accepted, assimilated. But if one is so busy doing and experiencing that he or she has no time for quiet reflection, then life becomes not a connected whole but a pile of beads without a string. We have to take time to withdraw from the transitory in order to discover the permanent.

What's in It for Me: Divinizing

Becoming aware that one has been divinized by Jesus Christ, invited into the Trinity family, is not the same as the self-aggrandizing divinization of Roman emperors. Rather it is a felt realization of the numinous presence of God not only all around us but *within* us. God is there all the time, waiting, but, like God's forgiveness, God's will to share the divine aliveness with us can't activate until we invite it. It is the heart-stopping understanding that, despite our short-comings, despite our seeming insignificance to most of those around us, the God who dwells in unapproachable light dwells within me.

On the one hand, relating personally to a God vaster than the universe takes a little doing. On the other, the Ancient of Days on a throne both risks becoming an idol and flies in the face of what we know about reality, that God inhabits a dimension beyond the limits of time and space: God has no beard, no throne, no right hand, no genitals. Yet I still have to deal with God, person-to-Person. Personally, I find a less unsatisfying answer in physics—or rather in *meta*physics; in "Einstein-plus."

Suppose there were a Reality faster than light; it would be everywhere at once, so super-energized that it would be at rest. And scientists now believe when they crack open the innermost kernel of the atom, it will be non-extended energy. Every object we see—though it appears rock-hard—is actually just another form of energy: $e = mc^2$. Couple that science with all we know from religion: encounters with God so often described as fiery bushes and pillars and tongues of flame. And realize that, when Moses asked Yahweh his name, the answer was: I am who am. God is the pool of energizing existence out of which everything draws its "is," "the living freshness deep-down things." It may not help everyone, but when I pray, I pray to a Person made of light.

This is an adaptation of a sufi meditation on light and God. Relax and get rid of all the in-charge-ness, then focus on a candle flame. Let your imagination draw a circle around it and expand the flame until it fills the whole circle. The light is like the invisible-but-truly-present atoms which bond the air and flame and candle. Then imagine the light swelling beyond the circle to fill the room. Then beyond the building, beyond the whole country, beyond the globe. And then beyond. Into the immeasurable Source of all light.

"The world is charged with the grandeur of God." So are you. Bow to the divine in you.

Choice or Chance?

Prayer is truly essential for ourselves and our children, not only as humans but as Christians. As human beings we need time to regain our inner stability, time to re-collect the self—not the vague and surface "I" of everyday life but the real "I." And the solitude that prayer demands lets us face our true selves without all the posturing and pretense that helps us bluff our way through the day. As Christians, too, we need prayer. Without real contact with the Person about whom the theological texts were written and whom the mass celebrates, is it any wonder the texts are no more meaningful than the insights of a dead rabbi and the liturgy no more involving than a long lunch for a Guest of Honor who never shows up?

There is no "only" way or time or place to pray. Like

Goldilocks, we have to try a lot of them to find which
"feels" best. Some find it best after work, after the dishes are
done, after the late news and before bed. Some like to sit
quietly; others prefer walking; still others contort themselves into a lotus. But the most important element is to have
a *focus* to come back to when you're distracted. And you
will be distracted. The body gurgles; limbs cramp; noses
itch; you suddenly remember, "I didn't call Sue!" The focus
brings you back to your center.

Anything will do: a crucifix, a candle, a rock. But some
of the most "professional" pray-ers in the world use a
mantra.

People say they don't say the rosary anymore "because I
never think of what the words of the prayers mean." That's
real left-brain, analytical, insight-mongering talk! The
whole *purpose* of the prayers, repeated over and over until
the words have no meaning, is to *short-circuit* that calculating intelligence! None of our conversations are worth re-
cording, but there is always a more important conversation
going on "underneath" the seemingly important one: "I
enjoy being-with you."

The Jesus Prayer is a mantra, too. On the long easy in-
take of breath: "Jesus, Son of David," and on the long easy
exhale: "have mercy on me, a sinner." You could do it with
any line you love: "And I, except You enthrall me, never
shall be free, nor ever chaste, except You ravish me." Just
being-with.

Others like to pray as St. Ignatius taught: applying all
the senses to a gospel scene so "You Are There," savoring
the brittle matzo and the tang of the wine, breathing the
sweat, kneeling and taking the disciples' feet into your
hands and washing them, feeling the texture of the skin.
Then looking up and seeing that those you work with have
taken the disciples' places.

But the critical difference between praying and merely clearing the mind is the "connection": from the beginning of the praying and consistently through it, being explicitly aware that Someone else is there—silent, perhaps, but there, the God whose faithfulness, and forgiveness, and fondness for us are forever.

That sure looks to me worth finding time for.

11

Understanding Sacraments

A feeling of awe came over the crowd when they saw
this, and they praised God for giving such power to
human beings.

—Matthew 9:10

A wise Zenmaster once wrote: "You must learn to understand the 'Ah!' of things!" Alas, few things make the
young say "Wow!" nowadays: a spectacular dive on "Wide
World of Sports," a great body, a Trans Am. The media have
successfully made the objectively trivial important and the
objectively important trivial. Thus, little chance teenagers
will find much "Ah!" in bread or wine or oil. We forgot the
taste of bread, unless it's slathered with peanut butter; wine
is nothing unless you have too much; oil is for salads and
suntans. And our Catholic symbolic rituals seem to the
young to have not the remotest resonance with other celebrations they are used to.

The Need for Symbol and Ritual

Most Catholic symbols sacred to me as a boy seem
drained of any effectiveness for today's young. I don't know

any students who wear a miraculous medal or a scapular or carry rosaries. And yet, because they're human, they do invest a "sacredness" in physical objects which somehow embody a reality which is not itself physical. A varsity jacket is only a coat, but made precious by a season of shared blood, sweat, and tears. The same is true of a senior ring (if you can afford one). A hashmark haircut makes a "statement," even if only, "Take *that!*" A driver's license, a car, a credit card "say" something important to someone who has yet to find an inner self. And on a wider scale, the effusion of yellow ribbons during the Gulf War shows that Americans are not yet entirely dulled to symbolism. That lone student motionless in front of behemoth tanks in Tiennamen Square says more of gallantry in helplessness than any treatise. Hearts can still be moved.

The young also have a hunger for communal symbolic ritual, though not explicitly aware of it. Something in us hankers for ritual to break the deadening routine and put our lives into a bigger context. Games begin with "The Star Spangled Banner," and even if it carries no sacredness most times, God help any corpulent comedienne who mocks it. When soldiers come home from the Gulf, there's *got* to be a parade, some concrete way to show the thanks we withheld from the boys of Vietnam. The Fourth of July would be just a day without the fireworks. And the Olympics begin with the torch and balloons and hoopla.

Reconnoiter before a direct approach to sacraments, show the meaning of symbol and ritual first from an unintimidating distance. List the symbols and rituals above and explore what society is trying to say *through* them, what they show about ourselves and our values, why we feel we need to express our intangible pride concretely. Then turn to the rituals and symbols integral to athletics and rock, which students know better than we, but whose messages and values they surely haven't analyzed.

Why such fuss over eleven overpaid grown men hauling an inflated pig bladder through eleven others on a big lawn with white stripes? Yet millions watch with the avidity of Saracens on jihad and argue referees' calls as meticulously as theologians at Nicea. Why is it important to watch garishly made-up, long-maned, skinny men in sadomasochistic drag, shrieking what seems gibberish to the uninitiate, trashing guitars, and exploding bombs?

Because it's *special*—in a world where "special" doesn't have any meaning anymore.

There might be the key. If Jules Verne transported one of the Waltons' children from the Depression to today, the child would be numbstruck. Luxuries and miracles all over the place! Wonderland! Wow! Yet today's teenagers simply take Wonderland for granted. Yawn! They don't realize how fortunate, perhaps even spoiled, even the poorest of them is, compared to a child fifty years ago—or to the over-whelming majority of children on the planet today. Nothing is "special," not for very long. A great many of our young today have become "junkies," looking for an ever more powerful jolt, because luxury became so commonplace.

Most have been scared away from drugs as a relief from the routine, mediocrity, disillusion, boredom of their ordinary days. But every week, the sit-coms' treatment of sexuality has to get a little bit bolder, MTV a bit more explicit, rap lyrics a bit more bestial. Not many realize rock 'n' roll got its name from a euphemism for sexual intercourse. Madonna understands that, if most of us don't. Like Hitler, she shrewdly guesses which way the parade is heading and, every time, gets in front of it.

Madonna is a perfect symbol of the needs of many of our young. Each time she ups the ante on the public's willingness to be shocked. She has nothing to hide, simply because there is nothing there: a gaudy manipulator who reduces life to one dimension, over which she has mistressful control. But she also answers needs in most of us; why else does she get so much coverage? That need in even the best of us is the restlessness of the Id within the corset of the Superego, the child in us yearning to fire the finger at parents and teachers and cops and just cut loose, as she does so slyly and slickly.

Sports and rock now ritualize violence and sex: the Id. Imagine Grandma Walton at a modern hockey game or sitting through "Truth or Dare." But like the ancient Romans we have come to accept slowly escalating violence and sex simply as givens; unless a performance is particularly brutal or blatant, we have lost our capacity to be shocked. Make the slightest critique about the glut of athletics in our lives and you risk being called an un-American priss; even hint that many rock lyrics are immoral and you get sneered down as a penny-ante Jesse Helms.

If all that is even to some extent true, anyone who tries to make the quiet, homely symbols of the sacraments meaningful to our present audience faces a labor not unworthy of Hercules.

Need for Religious Symbols and Rituals

But three moments in life demand religious symbol and ritual, when people who "don't need church" do need church, moments with too much "Ah!" in them for any other context than a religious one: birth, marriage, and death. When an infant is born, even if the parents don't practice, the child *has* to be baptized, not out of fear of hell but "because it's so *important!*" When two people vow unconditional responsibility for one another till death, it just doesn't "happen" in a J.P's office. And at the moment of a loved one's death, God is no longer escapable.

In teaching sacraments, begin with marriage, baptism, and dying, since the young can resonate to those needs, if their vague knowledge of those three great life-moments is brought to the surface. Start with what is meaningful to *them,* not what was meaningful to Hebrews two thousand years ago or medieval peasants or liturgists today. If they are to interiorize the value of Christian ritual, we must come at sacraments from the *inside,* not from the outside. Doctrines, quotes from councils, even scripture might be useful later, *ad complementum doctrinae.* But not at the outset, not with an audience few of whom have any sense of history, much less of historical symbolism, biblical allusions, and the ancient world's bewildering fascination with numerology. We're teaching quondam children, not graduate students.

As salespersons, capitalize on the audience we have, not treating sacraments in some dry discourse laced with allusions to documents they never read and never will. To see sacraments as valuable, they must seem valuable to the self-absorbed. Treat them, then, as moments of genuine personal *empowerment.*

Marriage is the easiest sacrament to explain because its motivation is easiest to understand. From the beginning, gear your pedagogy not to the neat logical development of the catechism but to the confused psychological development of the audience. Remember, too, that doctrinal battles are rarely derailed by faulty logic but almost always by faulty (biased) perception of the evidence. Once a student starts off on a too-narrow premise, he or she can argue in an impeccably linear way, so trying to derail that student then is as futile as convincing a mental patient the FBI isn't watching him through the TV set.

What's the difference between living together and marriage? Why is a "trial marriage" a contradiction? In the second act of "The Skin of Our Teeth," Maggie Antrobus, whose husband is going off with a floozie, gives the answer: "I didn't marry you because you were perfect, George. I didn't even marry you because I loved you. I married you because you gave me a promise. That promise made up for your faults. And the promise I gave you made up for mine. Two imperfect people got married, and it was that promise that made the marriage. . . . And when our children were growing up, it wasn't a house that protected them; and it wasn't our love that protected them—it was that promise."

A marriage is not a contract signed in an office; it is a commitment in the heart—surely not in the analytical mind!—to take responsibility for another person "all the days of my life." You can't "try out" a permanent promise.

Come at the symbols that attempt to embody a marriage meditatively rather than preceptively. What does a promise really mean? And what does it mean taken in front of a couple hundred people, and "before God"? What do rings "say"—senior ring, bishop's ring, Frodo's ring? Rings bespeak both constriction and empowerment. Before this moment, each was free to choose from all the single members of their opposite sex. But that freedom couldn't activate until *expended* on the one, rejecting all the rest. And a ring is a reminder that one is never free of responsibility for the other, but also that one is never alone.

Baptism usually brings up a lot of false problems: "What right did they . . . ?" The problem is the "club" image of the church: "Why was I committed to membership in a club—*and* its dues—before I checked it out?" But it's easier to make a choice when you have something to contrast the alternatives against. And if Catholicism were precious to parents, it would actually be *un*kind of them not to share it. Now you're old enough to assess what baptism means and decide for yourself if you want to accept it. Just don't trash an ugly antique before appraising it.

To be frank, I believe baptism is more for the parents and godparents than for the child. I find enormous difficulty thinking it has anything whatever to do with sin. When I look at an infant, making sucky-kissy noises, a being who can't control its own bowels yet, I can't accept that it is responsible for anything, nor can I love a "God" who would in any way reprehend such an innocent as guilty of a "debt." Sin is about death; baptism is about life. It is a public acknowledgment that this child is more important than a mere animal cub, more important even than a merely human being. This child has been invited into the Trinity family, and this moment tries to physicalize that belief for the child's parents: This child will never really die.

Like oil, water is impoverished as a symbol for American children, in contrast to even today's mideastern children. We take for granted an endless supply for our cooking, washing, showers, pools, lawns. To "reactivate" water's symbolic power, turn first not to the Bible, but to science. Pull back and look at an earthrise. What makes our planet different? After all our exploration, ours is still the only blue one we know. Where did everything emerge from? The sea was the first womb, and for nine months we floated in our own mother's wombs, and our bodies are seventy percent water. A human can survive without food for over a month, but only five days without water. Over the womb-like font, the priest shows that this child's mother risked death to bring it into the light, and Jesus endured death to bring it into still newer life. Then, if it helps to understand better, place this moment against the waters of chaos, the flood, crossing the Red Sea. What did all those water-moments mean? Starting over.

Oil, for me, is too tough. I explain about anointing kings, knights, champions, but I can't find a way to make it genuinely meaningful to kids for whom oil is what you put in a car. If you can, I'd be grateful to hear how.

The priest gives the parents a lighted candle. What does fire mean? What does it offer our daily lives? Light, warmth, security. What does a firebrand mean? What connection has that to what being a Christian really means? Think of all the times you remember fire occurring in the Hebrew scriptures and in the gospels. What does it mean in all those places? Empowerment. Now why would the church offer an infant fire at baptism?

The child receives a new white gown. Who else wears white? Nurses, doctors, missionaries. Why? What does white "say"?

Why do the parents supply two "new" parents? "Well, if the parents die . . ." But there's a bigger reason. (Wait them out!) Is it possible the godparents are also symbols? That they stand for *more* than just themselves? Some kind of *second* family?

Sickness and Death. Except for those who have lost a parent or sibling, most kids have been both overexposed to death and shielded from it. On the one hand, before kindergarten they've watched more deaths than a veteran in the army of Genghis Khan; they know all the dead got up and got paid; small children see no difference between real deaths on the news and faked ones on cop shows. On the other hand, many have never been to a funeral or even a wake, to a hospital or nursing home; the sick and dying do it "somewhere else"; parents try to protect them from that, and thus protect them from becoming adult human beings.

Thus, the first task is to make them aware of—and *own* —the fact that suffering is a given in human life. For all their parents' protectiveness, it *will* come, and shielding

them from that fact of life is no kindness. Without surmounting suffering, we remain babies for life. And at least
by high school, adolescents must also own the fact of their
own inevitable, unpredictable deaths, to make them see that
their days are a finite number and thus too precious to fritter
away. Meditate on it, understand it, take possession of it.
Until then, it is impossible to make them honestly understand not only the value of the sacrament of healing but the
value of *anything.*

Atheists believe that, since there can be no reality
beyond the here and now, death is a period. We stop being
real. But that means that all the struggles—and the dignity
we achieve from overcoming them—are wiped out as if
they had never been. At death, Mother Teresa and Times
Square pimps get exactly the same "reward": annihilation.
Contemplate that a while. Then you might begin to understand why, when a family member is dangerously ill, someone inevitably says, "Send for the priest." Both the victim
and the family have to put this shattering event into some
kind of context where it has meaning. As young people often say to me at a teenager's funeral, "Help me make sense
of this."

As Job discovered, the worst part is not the physical
pain but the not-knowing: the helplessness, depression,
even despair. It's so unfair; what have I done to deserve
this—not just my own pain but the pain I see on the faces of
people I love?

Perhaps the presence of the priest himself is more
meaningfully sacramental than his actions or prayers or oils.
He is the embodiment of our belief. Somehow he "says" we
know God must have a purpose in suffering and death; otherwise nothing we do has any purpose at all. His presence
"says" we know Jesus went through all this, too, to show us
not only that it is inevitable but also how to do it well. One

of the most appealing aspects of Christianity is that it is the only religion whose God was also tempted to despair: "My God! My God! Why have you abandoned me?" But then he said, "Into your hands I commend my spirit," yielding to his Father. The sacrament of healing is a channel by which Jesus empowers us to do what he did: die and survive.

The sacrament of healing is not some kind of Wild West medicine show, promising miraculous healing of the body. It is rather a healing of the soul which separates us from beasts, healing the bitterness, the fear, the loneliness. The ritual puts this agonizing event into the context where it does have meaning: eternity. Although within our this-world cocoons the suffering appears enormous, in the context of eternity it is a labor pain from which new life will emerge. One of the holiest men I've met, a merchant seaman dying alone of cancer and TB, said it most eloquently: "Yes, it is very difficult. But isn't it wonderful God trusts me enough to give it to me?"

Reconciliation. No one looks forward to confronting the dentist because we have short memories and "the short view." We forget how good it feels when it's over, running our tongues around teeth that are "brand new again." We also forget the buoyancy when we walk away from an honest, cards-on-the-table confession, "brand new again," empowered to start fresh again.

As only recent graduates from childhood, adolescents have an irritatingly short view. Even in solving made-up moral dilemmas, they ferret out the loopholes and go for the utilitarian solution rather than the alternative that would make them persons of integrity and character. No matter what the personality type, guilt trips are a bummer. The reason is that responsibility, gratitude, and accountability are limits on a freedom they have been led (somehow) to believe is without limits. Therefore, since hell is out of fashion as a motive, the first task is to engender a genuine sense of the reasonableness and value of guilt. Without guilt, what you get is Auschwitz, Central Park gang rapes, non-addicted pushers, saturation bombing, toxic waste dumps, mob hitmen, terrorists, and the list goes on.

"It's too embarrassing to tell my sins to a priest. Why can't I just go out and confess them directly to God?" Fine. When was the last time you *did* it? And the doctor who treats herself has a fool for a patient. Unless you tell someone else, you either let yourself off too easily or the bottled up guilt builds till it explodes. Telling someone else gets it out there on the table, without mincing words, without self-protectiveness. And the priest reaches out and *touches* you: "Welcome. I'm a sinner, too." The priest has been trained to help, to tell you when you might be kidding yourself or even too hard on yourself.

When I hear confessions, I always end, "Well, you're a good man, aren't you? You're a fine woman." Invariably, the penitent blushes and says, "I hope so" or "I try" or "You don't really know me." I have to tell them bad people don't confess. Only good people do. And they've come, so they must be "good people." Also, I never give "prayer penances," always "do penances"; better to show a bit of love than rattle off a few Hail Marys: "When you go home, say, 'Mom, is there anything I could do for you before I . . . ?' She'll faint, but you'll both be happier."

Eucharist. Mass is usually so sedate it's often sedative. The congregation's role is mostly passive: the priest "says" the mass; the faithful "receive." "*Grex,*" the root of "congregation," even means a herd of sheep. Youngsters know "special" celebrations like awards banquets, Christmas, weddings, but mass is definitely not "special" to them. Our culture encourages them to develop not only fast food tummies but also fast food minds. As with all the sacraments, our basic job is to sensitize minds insensitive to nuance.

Because mass is so non-involving for them, teenagers ask the wrong questions about it: "Why do I have to? I don't get anything *out* of it!" That's ingrate talk. The meaning of the word "eucharist" is "thanksgiving." So in order to find any meaning in it one has to feel lucky and grateful for gifts one did nothing to deserve.

Blind-side them before you even begin to discuss the eucharist. Have them list all the people they care for, name-by-name. When that's dwindled down, list all the things they like at home, in their neighborhoods, at school. When that's done, ask who invited you into all that? Believe it or not, for billions of years the world got along without you. Your parents didn't *have* to have you; they could have had a swimming pool and a lot fewer headaches instead. And where did your parents come from—all the way back to your great^{nth}-grandparents trundling along on their knuckles? Take a look at those lists again. If God opened the door and invited you to this party, and all he asks is forty-five minutes a week, what kind of person are you if you say, "Get lost"?

What are our souls hungry for? This meal empowers us to go on striving. As the madwoman says in *The Man on a Donkey,* "Think of it, Wat! God, in a bit of bread, come to bring morning into the darkness of our bellies!" The priest breaks up the bread and passes it around. What does that "say" about what we should do with ourselves? As with the miracle of the loaves, the more you give away, the more you have left over. At the consecration of the wine, the priest says, "It will be shed for you, and for all, *so that* sins may be forgiven. Do this in memory of me." Not just offer the cup, but forgive sins. In the 1960s, some well-meaning ninnies celebrated "mass" with hamburgers and beer since, as bread and wine were staples for Jesus' people, they are for ours. Why is that "wrong"? Because it's not "special."

The very gathering of people "says" something: We may not know one another, but by God we're here. We stand for something. The fact that you are all here, too, helps my unbelief. It empowers me to go on, knowing I'm not a lonely fool.

Confirmation. When I dream of being pope for a day, one of my first acts is to decree that no one be confirmed until age eighteen and only after personally requesting it. There would be more in the ritual of the *Ruah Yahweh,* the whirlwind of Job, and the fiery gusts of Pentecost! I toy with a ukase of a week-long retreat in the wilderness beforehand, and I'd surely reinstate the slap—and a good hard belt at that. Primitive cultures knew far more how important a definitive rite of passage is. And the ritual would explicitly contain an acceptance of the invitation puberty has presented the emergent adult to leave childhood behind and take on a new role in the church: empowered as a healer and apostle.

I sigh to admit it's a pipedream. But I do believe youngsters being trained for confirmation should be forced to understand that this is not just the bishop, in the name of the church, confirming the child as an acceptable member. The child, too, is confirming an acceptance of the church, of his or her baptism, and of his or her mission as an active healer and apostle. It is not only a commission but a *commitment.* (Unfortunately, I know few if any twelve year olds can comprehend that. At that age, commitment is as incomprehensible as sex. Thus the pipedream.)

It took me too long to see that the seven gifts of the Spirit "bestowed" in confirmation are not gifts at all. If I received knowledge, understanding, wisdom, prudence, courage, reverence and awe, then why am I still so relent-lessly dumb, befuddled, misguided, rash, cowardly, disre-spectful, and dull? The answer is that those gifts are not gifts but challenges to actuate those potential powers. I've never seen them explained that way.

Ordination. Each of the sacraments is an "ordination," an empowerment to a larger office in the community or to keep us going in the right direction together as a people for others.

When I preside at a couple's conferral of marriage on one another, I stand down in the aisle between the couple and the people, because for me that sums up the function of the ministerial priest: to act as a "lens" between the couple and the people, who *are* the church. The couple submit their vows not to my blessing but to the blessing of the church. So I ask the church, if it approves of this union, to signify their approval by applauding as loudly as they can. (They never let me down.)

That is as good an example as any of all the functions of the priest: to be a lens between the people and God, trying to focus their hopes to God and God's faithfulness back to them. And one can never forget that the root-meaning of "minister" is not "director" or "thinking-substitute"; the root is "servant."

At an ordination, not just the bishop but all the priests press their hands on the top of the ordinand's head. What does that "say"? The priest-to-be lays his own hands on the book of gospels and on the vessels used at mass? Why? Why is he anointed with oil? Why are priests set apart as celibates?

Perhaps then young people can at least vaguely grasp that Jesus himself is the sacrament of sacraments: the embod-iment of the invisible God, and the crucifix embodies God's will for us as Christians. Perhaps they can understand a bit more that the church is the continuing embodiment of Christ: Jesus is the head, the Spirit is our soul, and we are the parts. Jesus has no hands without our hands, no hearts but our hearts. His Spirit within us empowers us to live far greater lives than we had ever dared to imagine.

12

Practica Quaedam

"Remember, I am sending you out like sheep among wolves; so be cunning as serpents yet as harmless as doves."

—Matthew 10:16

And truer words were never spoken!

(1) *Who You Are*

You are not merely a pedagogue. You are a salesperson. Unlike *any* other discipline in a Catholic school, your department is not merely in the business of imparting knowledge. You are in the business of eliciting agreement with what you claim to be the truth. Every time you sense resistance in your audience, you are getting through. That's when the real struggle begins. If you don't get them upset, you might as well go talk to orangutans in the zoo.

(2) *Your Real Goal*

They will not remember too much of what you say; they will remember who you were in their lives. At any particular moment, they may think of you as a hard-hearted son (or daughter) of a bitch. That's the "short view." You have always to keep the long view; remember Annie Sullivan and Helen Keller.

Your main goal is to teach them to *reason,* honestly. The religious problems they are going to face haven't even been invented yet, or at least they haven't become real for *them* yet (and that's the only real that's really real). What you have to do is make them uncomfortable with easy answers.

Real education means learning how to learn, and it takes *consistent* effort to discover how to deal with ever more complex data and relationships. Real education means learning:

(a) to be curious, to distrust what "everybody knows," to smell rats;

(b) to be humble before the evidence, no matter down what unpleasant paths the evidence may lead;

(c) how to think: not just have thoughts, but to *reason:*
   1. gather the data,
   2. sift the data to find what's essential,
   3. put the best data into some kind of logical sequence (an outline) so you can
   4. draw a conclusion and
   5. put the conclusion out to be critiqued.

(d) how to care for the people around you;

(e) the courage to stand up and be counted.

Photocopy this outline and paste it over your desk! If you can "only" do that, you won't have failed.

It's not data they memorize that's important. Most of what they remember will be useless, and what they can't remember they can always go to a library and look up. What we challenge them to do—or ought to—is to challenge themselves: to wrestle with ever more complex data, honestly, fairly, no matter the cost.

Every time you give the swamp-gas essay a 70, every time you allow some kid to copy on a quiz, every time you look the other way, *you* are the enemy.

(3) *The Real Audience*—and Your Expectations of Them
If you want to wash out your starry-eyed idealism right away (and that's wise!), pose them the following dilemma: "On your tenth birthday, your parents bought you a dog you named Rags. She's been with you ever since: waited for you at the school bus stop, slept at the end of your bed, sensed your moods. Now: this crazy zillionaire comes and says that he'll pay your way through college *and* guarantee you a job starting at $70,000 *if* you'll toss Rags off the edge of a cliff. Don't answer too quickly. That's a lot of bucks, and Rags is getting pretty old." I'm guessing that the results will be rather sobering, if they synchronize with mine. But better to know the audience to whom you bring the message. That way, you can adapt your approach to the audience you're trying to convince.

Take them where they *are*, not where you'd like them to be or where your college profs suggested they might be. Kohlberg says that, in the normal scheme of things, most of them are either in Stage One (fear), Stage Two (hope of self-aggrandizement), or Stage Three (loyalty to small groups like the gang or family). Some few are (perhaps) in Stage Four (loyalty to a larger group like the church or the nation). Personally, I distrust that. It seems they are often being loyal to their parents when they seem to be loyal to the church or nation.

No matter what their external personality type—jock, flirt, effeminate, anonymous—you can count on the fact that they are self-absorbed, and the self-absorption is teflon-coated. And if you teach in New York City, it's five inches thick! Don't confuse their narcissism with self-love; it is precisely the opposite: self-distaste which is so strong that it masks itself as its opposite. Narcissism is the need to disguise the shortcomings so that, even to the self, there is no need to apologize even for wrongs for which one is genuinely guilty. I *must* feel OK about myself, even when I have no right to feel OK.

Most well-intentioned parents have only two basic commands written on their "Parental Superego": (1) Protect them from harm, and (2) Give them the best you can. Such parents don't realize that both of those seemingly admirable goals prevent their children from becoming human adults. If they face no suffering, they can't achieve dignity. If they are given the best, they begin to believe the best is a given.

If you start out with the belief that these are Christian children you are teaching, you might as well go make change in Woolworth's. They are baptized, but they have never undergone the agony of Christian conversion—nor should they be expected to have done that. Nor is your job to convert them, but only to make them *less unready* for conversion than they were before you came along. Your job is to get them ready for the minefield their parents are often too protective to prepare them for.

Don't get me wrong! They're good kids; they're wonderful kids. If they weren't, I wouldn't still be doing this after thirty years. But they're *kids*. Don't let any course you have ever taken blind you to that—especially not any education courses, which are taught by people whose only hands-on contact with adolescents is with their teenage nieces and nephews.

If you pitch your course to the lowest common denominator, the pagans with Christian labels, you do no harm to the genuine Christians and altruists. Substantiate your claims by sheer *reason*. As much as you can, back up your claims with references to psychology, physics, sociology, rather than only scripture and tradition; students can't argue with them. Not only will you do no harm to the already-convinced, you will in fact give them a rational apologetic with which to counter the atheists, cynics, and opportunists in the inevitable college dorm debates. Since they are, by reason of their normal developmental stage, self-absorbed, work on their self-interest—their self-esteem—in being moral, worshiping, helping the neighbor. "How can you feel good about yourself unless you do?"

Make clear, again and again, that when you demolish one of their opinions, you are not demolishing *them*.

Set your expectations low enough that you can treasure the *small* things: "Not a half-bad class; I was arguing with my friend, and she really liked what you say; we both know you're right, but I just can't give it up." When a scientist goes into her lab at Sloan-Kettering, she doesn't expect to find the cure for cancer by the end of the semester. She's just edging closer to an answer. So, too, with us.

(4) *Discipline*

I learned my best lesson in discipline from my dad. Back in the Cro-Magnon era when I was in high school, you didn't come back at ten in the morning from a prom. I got home from one at 1:30 in the morning. My dad greeted me at the door in his bathrobe; I'd never even seen my dad in a bathrobe before! He looked me straight in the eye and said, in this quiet voice, "I *never* want you to bring a girl home at one in the morning. Do . . . you . . . understand that?" And he turned and walked away. I wanted him to *hit* me! But there was no way I could argue with that quiet, intimidating, moral self-assurance. So when somebody does something unworthy, go to the side of his or her desk, and in a voice no one else can hear, say, "I don't want that again. Do you understand me?'' Nothing is more intimidating than quiet resolve.

Don't *ever* raise your voice. There's no place further you can go after that. If it becomes commonplace, they'll develop an immunity to it.

Don't *ever* send a student to detention. That's like saying, "You wait till your father gets home." The students sense a weakness in teachers who can't handle their own problems. Deal with consistent troublemakers one-on-one, not in the public forum. That's one of the major reasons they're making trouble: to get attention they can't merit any other way.

And remember the saying of Fr. Flanagan of Boystown: "There's no such thing as a bad boy (or girl)." Hurt, maybe; confused, angry, perhaps even sick. But never bad.

One day a boy who was often in error but never in doubt, at the end of an acrimonious "debate," muttered, "Up there pontificating all the time." I said to him, "Joe, by Monday, I want you to write me a two-page essay (A) telling me what 'pontificating' really means, and (B) making your best case that I do in fact stand up there and say things without the evidence to back them up." A month later, he still hadn't handed it in. But every time I saw him I kept asking for it.

When they blow off at you, most often they're angry not at you but at themselves. Make sure you stop them and force them to see that, to focus the anger where it ought to be. Make them realize that you have feelings, too. That's part of the job.

There are teachers who use draconian methods on cheating: ripping up the bluebook, etc. Far better when you see one trying to cheat to say to the class, "Don't show too much interest in your neighbor's progress." They all get it, and he or she will blush. That's enough. Or go to the offender and whisper in her ear, "In a week you're going to forget you even took this test. Is a couple of points really worth your sense of integrity?" Instead of blowing the situation out of proportion, show it up for the embarrassingly petty thing it is.

Similarly, when a student consistently shows on quizzes that he or she hasn't read the material, write on the top, "Don't you have any self-esteem, Chris?"

The key to discipline is fairness and self-confidence. Oddly, in the beginning, we're so bent on succeeding that we forget they're *kids*. Granted that there are thirty of them and one of you, and they could murder you and devour the evidence, but they won't. If you have a consistent problem —say, constant side-comments on what you say, stop the class in its tracks and say, "Okay. Let's talk. I'm just not going to take this crap any longer."

(5) *Governance*

There is a spectrum of methods of governing, from the totalitarian to the individualist. Totalitarians get the railroads to run on time; individualists allow for a profusion of creativity. But victims of totalitarian governance become spiritless, and victims of individualist governance become spineless. You are the adult: the hard place against which they hone their new-found adulthood. Tough love is the oxymoron that best describes the balance between the two extremes.

If you lose your temper, apologize—publicly. It's worth the minor embarrassment to preserve your *own* self-esteem as well as your credibility. What's more, vulnerability is an approach they're not used to from adults. If they "get" you on a loophole, concede—but plug the loophole the next time. This year I asked for a term paper five pages long. One student handed in a paper that was four pages,

inch-and-a-half margins all round and printed on a com-
puter in quarter-inch type. Next year, the assignment sheet
will read: "One-inch margins all around; use a type font no
larger than the type on this page."

(6) *Epistemology*

Whatever you skip, don't skip the class on epistemology—and at the very beginning of the year. You can depend
on it from there on. When someone makes an egregious
claim, ask: "Where's your evidence? Your opinion is *only* as
good as the evidence that backs it up." And on papers, keep
splashing red *"EVIDENCE!"* Perhaps the subject matter
you're teaching won't seem "real" to them now, but when
it does, you'll have taught them how to reason to their own
answers.

Avoid dogma. Nothing turns them off more than hypocrisy and smugness (although a few of the most turned-off are
experts at both). Claim nothing more than a high degree of
probability for the existence of God, the superiority of Catholicism, or the immorality of extra-marital intercourse.
All dogma does is send them in search of chinks. Of course
there are chinks. We have human minds, not divine minds.
Claiming certitude is blasphemy.

On my classroom wall, I have sayings on poster paper,
like a Dickensian workhouse. If I happen to be boring them
at the moment, they just might pick up something. And they
do. One of them is: "The great sin is certitude. The great
virtue is doubt." Without doubt, you can never learn, never
go in search of better answers than those that contented you
so far.

(7) *Schedule*

On the first day of the quarter or trimester, hand out a
schedule listing what papers are due what day, quizzes,

tests. It takes a lot of time, but it has more than a few advantages. First, it forces *you* to know where the course is beginning, where it is heading; it will never be "What did we do yesterday?" We owe that to kids. Second, you can fend off "When's the quiz?" with "That's why I wrote the schedule: so I don't have to answer questions like that." Third, they have no excuses when the test comes around that they didn't have time to study; they've "known" about it for four weeks.

And put your grading rules on that first sheet they see; you'll never regret it when they start complaining at the end of the marking period. In my courses, I usually have at least ten reaction papers each quarter, which are worth fifty points on the final grade. Therefore, each paper is worth five points. There is no grade on the paper, but they know from my comments that they didn't get full credit ("Pretty skimpy" means minus one; "This wasn't worth writing or reading, was it?" means minus two). Better-than-average pages I write, "Good page, Red," and add a point; really terrific pages I write, "Helluva page!" and add two. The deadline on the due date is 2:45 when I leave the school for play practice. Every school day the paper is late, minus one point; after five days, forget it. This means you ask the attendance officer for the daily printout of absentees. It's a bit of a hassle, but it has an amazing effect on tardy papers.

(8) *"Religion"*

If I were king, I'd abolish the title "religion class" or even "religious studies" for "theology." As the text says, theology is what you know, belief is what you accept, religion is what you do. Saints can fail theology; the only way you can fail religion is to go to hell.

If you ask an opinion question like "What do you think of me?" and they answer, "I think you're an arrogant pig," they get full grades; they've answered your question. All you can grade is the thoroughness of their evidence and reasoning for arriving at that unflattering conclusion. Whatever the title of the department, make sure students know that your quizzes and tests are not tests of their *beliefs,* but only if they know what the text and classes have claimed and why. No problem if they disagree, as long as they know what you've *said.*

Make sure, from the start, they know that it is a definite possibility that one can flunk theology, and don't be afraid to do it. Love means saying, "I know you hate me right now, but I care about you so much I'm willing to take that."

(9) *Method*

The catechist's job is *not* to outline the text; that's *their* job, and on their own time. Unlike other courses, this one tries to elicit acceptance, not just knowledge. Therefore, you have to spend at *least* as much time on the gimmick that hooks their interest as you do on the content of the class. Presume they'd rather feed their parents to piranhas than listen to you, and you'll have a chance. Always start at an unintimidating distance from your real point. Jesus did that with the lawyer who asked what "neighbor" meant; had he given a direct answer, the lawyer would have gone away in disgust. So Jesus hooked him with the story of the good Samaritan. Do the same. Begin with a riddle: You don't see me, do you? "Of course, we do!" No, all you see is my body; the real me you have to make educated guesses about.

I begin every new unit with a survey of ten statements, asking for agreement or disagreement on the matter the unit is going to cover, just to stir up the sludge, e.g., Actresses like Glenn Close rightly receive smaller salaries than actors like Tom Cruise; In a race at a summer camp, a handicapped person should be given a head start, etc. I write down the numbers for each class; that tells them I'm really paying attention and it also helps me know where they stand. Don't comment on the "wrong" answers, unless they're a matter of objective fact. That's what the class is supposed to do.

Periodically, I also give no-name questionnaires like the one in Chapter 7 on sin, work, attitudes toward school, etc. Again, it lets them voice their opinions, tells them I'm interested in what they think, and lets me know just what that is.

(10) *Reaction Papers*

At least once a week, give a reaction paper on the subject of the present unit. We are not just indoctrinators; we are trying to elicit acceptance. They can say anything they want (tactfully) as long as they back it up with evidence and honest reasoning. It takes time to read and comment on them (I give fifty a year to one hundred students; that's four thousand papers, and this is my twenty-fifth year teaching theology: that's a Guinness Record, for sure). But it's the best thing I've done as a teacher. First, it forces them to focus an opinion; they learned by fifth grade that the grandstanders will ask all the questions, and if she questions you, all you've got to do is stare at the rug long enough and she'll go to someone else. Second, although they may have some vague notions about the topic, if they haven't focused opinions into words, they don't *know* them. Third, it offers the opinion to someone more knowledgeable, who cares, and who's willing to point out things they might have overlooked. But most importantly it lets me know what I'm up against.

Comment on every page, and be sure to personalize it by using the student's name. But make sure you pose your comments most often in the form of questions: "Doesn't this contradict what you said on p. 15, Joe?" On the one hand, you want to make them keep thinking; on the other hand, you might be wrong when you write, "You didn't think much about this, Jean." Better to tack a "did you?" on the end.

After a while, you can tell pretty well when reaction papers are just words filling space: a half-page of wind. When they're only a few lines, write, "This wasn't worth writing or reading, right, Eddie?" If you occasionally get a paper that's insulting or even obscene, don't take it to the principal. Don't reply with equal rage. Rather, write something like, "Do you really think this is fair, Randy? Clever?" or better yet: "Wanna talk about this, Randy?"

(11) *Arguments*

Nobody argues with the physics or math teachers. But they will argue with you, because you're trying to alter their belief, attitudes, behavior. At times, admitting you're right will mean they ought to give up things they like very, very much. But at least you've gotten their attention.

The toughest ones are those who are hard-nosed: arrogantly ignorant. Remember that, when you get to questions about welfare or homosexuality, most often you're not arguing with the student but with his or her father. Most students' opinions are not their own at all but lifted "off the rack" from parents or TV and get a "personal" label slapped on them, as if the student actually had gathered the data, sifted it, put it into logical sequence to form an opinion and put it out to be critiqued. Keep reminding yourself to ask, "Where's your *evidence?*" And one or two anecdotes are not proof, nor is, "I saw this TV program once." When they dig in their heels like balky mules and just won't let the subject drop, say: "I beg you to entertain at least the possibility— the *possibility*—that you might be wrong."

The arrogantly ignorant honestly *resent* the fact that

you know more than they do, that you have in fact reasoned your way to your conclusions and they haven't. That's the reason they keep deriding "those guys who have their noses in a book all day long" and keep insisting that experience is the best teacher. Well, you've had more experience than they have, too. So have the writers of all the books they haven't read.

As the previous chapter said, most arguments are twisted not by faulty logic but by too-narrow perception of the evidence.

Kids are not the only ones who play the Maximize/Minimize Game: pump up the arguments that support my side and belittle anything that threatens it. Talk to tobacco experts about the effects of smoking, residents along the San Andreas Fault about earthquakes, carmakers about pollution. Early and often, write on the board: "VESTED INTEREST" and explain what it means.

I personally have a real problem in arguments with students which I really have to start doing something about. I jump in too quickly. This is my twenty-fifth year teaching three or four classes of the same material; I'm pretty sure I've heard it all; I can tell what the next sentence is going to be! The one about the guys with their noses in a book all day: "Look, not *all* day. That's not fair." "*See!* You never listen to us." Atticus Finch taught me that you've got to climb inside the other person's skin and walk around in it a while. But I forget. Many times what they say is ludicrous, but love says you listen, not because what they're saying is important, but because they're important.

I salve my conscience by saying they have the reaction papers to get off their opinions. But many of those are top-of-the-head; the issue has currency at the moment—especially if it threatens their behavior; even if I've heard it a thousand times (and I have), this is their first time.

But, like the war in Northern Ireland, arguments about religion are often not about finding the truth but rather about dominance. When that becomes clear—and I still haven't blown my stack—then I say, "Wait a minute, Marty. Do you want to find the truth, or do you just want to hang O'Malley's shorts up the flagpole?" The sly smiles tell you you're right.

One of the best classes I have each year (which I purloined from the superlative "Ethics in America" on PBS) is one where I role-play being a fifteen year old girl who is having a delirious affair with a thirty year old man. I keep insisting, "No. Don't say, 'I'd tell her . . .' I'm the girl. Tell *me.*" Well, they're all over me! After a while, I say, "Wait a minute! I brought this to you because I was so happy. I thought, after what you say about that big-mouthed priest and how you fight him about pre-marital sex, you'd *understand!*" It's *delicious!* When I'm role-playing, I can dodge their trenchant arguments! I can refuse to argue sequentially! I can even say, "I'm not going to listen to you anymore!" And at the end, I can say, "That's just the way *you* guys argue!" Again, the sly smiles. They learned.

(12) *The Enneagram*

You will have all kinds of personality differences in any class. I have found it a great help to use the Enneagram, nine basic personality types. In fact, I take two weeks with the seniors on it, and almost all of them find it valuable—even the somnabulists in the period after lunch. It is too complex to go into here, but there are many good books on it: Don Richard Riso, *Personality Types* (Houghton Mifflin) is the clearest. Also, Helen Palmer, *The Enneagram* (Harper & Row) and Beesing-Nogosek-O'Leary, *The Enneagram: A Journey of Self-Discovery.*

(13) *"I'm Lazy"*

I'm constantly astonished how many kids with impoverished vocabularies use the word "procrastinate"—and they know how to *spell* it, too! Perhaps because they've heard it and seen it on deficiency reports so often. There is *no* kid who is lazy. Just look at the handball courts during recess. Just look at a Friday night dance. If I told my boys that Miss Centerfold was down in the gym parading around in the dishabille with which she won her fleeting fame, my hunch is they could overcome their inertia and amble down for a viewing.

Kids aren't lazy, just unmotivated. If you could just find a *reason* for what they're asked to do—one meaningful to *them*—you'd have no trouble.

The quick-to-the-lip motive is "You need an education to get a good job." Nope. Check the Almanac: only twenty-five percent of American males and seventeen percent of females have completed college—and yet most of them are gainfully employed. Frank Sinatra never finished high school; neither did Peter Jennings. Then there has to be a better reason. There is: learning to think about ever more complex data. Every time you write the ten-minute swamp-gas essay, every time you copy a lab, every time you ask for an extension, you throw money away.

One motivation that gets to students (though they'd never admit it) is that they're subsidized to the tune of about fifteen grand a year: food, shelter, clothing, heat, insurance, etc. Not to give an honest day's work for that honest day's pay is grand larceny! Remember that when they bring up welfare cheats.

(14) *Little-League Narcissism*

Keep remembering they're still children. But also remember that it's our job to help cure them of that! What wears teachers down (it sure wears *me* down) is the seem-ingly endless number of thoughtless acts and omissions ado-lescents are ingeniously capable of: "Anybody got a pen?"; the heads down on the desk; the wise-ass side comments; the fact that they're used to talking when they watch videos at home.

If it helps at all, remember that Jesus—the greatest teacher who ever lived—had constantly to put up with "You can't really mean that" and "Are you going to restore the kingdom to Israel *now?*"

Practically, don't allow pen or paper borrowing. Only you will do that. And rent the pen to them for fifty cents each time; sell bluebooks for a dollar apiece. Let 'em fall asleep; then creep up beside them and bang the waste-basket. Turn on the lights and say, "If anybody wants to talk, leave."

(15) *Simplisms from TV*

Your greatest competitor is the television. What it says is beyond dispute. In order to undercut that, assign students to talk to real police, real lawyers, real doctors, real parents, and ask if the TV shows are even remotely like reality. Show them "Network." It's worth the three classes or so just to put some question marks in their minds about the Enemy's credibility.

(16) *The "Atheists"*

In my experience, the students who claim to be atheists adopt that stance for all the wrong reasons: bitterness against parents (or God), the boring mass, "all those rules." They haven't actually reasoned their way to atheism: gath-ered the data, etc. But I also find that they are generally very polite about it. They're open to reason. Then use that. I have a book called *Meeting the Living God* (Paulist) which has been pretty successful with self-claimed atheist students.

(17) *Children of Divorce*

More and more, nearly half our classes are children of divorce. When the topic comes up in class, we have to speak very gingerly about it. The wisest course seems to be stressing the importance of what a couple does before the relationship gets to a point where divorce seems the only rational alternative. From the outset, a couple ought to be more than careful before jumping into a permanent relationship with only their hearts. Like the act of faith, marriage is a *calculated* risk. But I don't think a teacher ought to shy away from saying that many divorces are caused by self-absorption. The best way to handle the pain that children who are victims of divorce undergo is to help them achieve a positive result from surmounting it.

(18) *"How'm I Doin'?"*

You'll get some indication of how you are doing by their quizzes, tests, and reaction papers, but don't let that be your *sole* indicator. If you did, you'd swallow a gas pipe. More and more in recent years, kids think they can simply get away with the absolute minimum. And in many cases they're dead right, especially if the administration depends on the parents for money and doesn't want them upset. But their kids will get a diploma without getting an education.

One way is to pass out the following sheet a week *after* the first marking period's grades have come out:

SUMMARY OF LAST QUARTER   **NAME** _____

Text and Printouts
_____ I really studied, underlined, took notes, etc.

_____ I read them pretty thoroughly
_____ I skimmed them
_____ I read them here and there
_____ I didn't read them

Notes
_____ I take thorough notes in almost every class
_____ I take down what you put on the board
_____ I rarely if ever take notes

Reaction Papers
_____ I really spend "quality time" on them, alone
_____ Sometimes I put in effort, the rest of the time not
_____ I just try to get them out of the way
_____ I genuinely want to learn to think for myself
The grade I honestly deserved last quarter: _____

If you emphasize that this can't possibly affect grades already history, most will be honest, and you have an indicator if their poor performance is due to you (and you ought to see the chair for some help) or if it is simply that they're not working (and you should turn your imagination to ways to get them to do that). Also, if you have students who check all the "rarely" items and yet also "I genuinely want to learn to think for myself," you have material for a bit of one-on-one dialogue.

The Absolutely Inevitable Statements

—"*We* heard *all this before!*"

Great! Then let's have a quiz. Then give them a half-sheet on all the things you were going to say in that class. What they say is usually true, at least to the extent that they were in the room when certain things were said. But they didn't *hear* them, not as they do when they hear, "You've got two cavities." Often they won't remember what you had them *memorize* last week! *Repetitio est mater studiorum.*

— *"Yeah, but if she wants it as much as you do . . ."*
     If she pleaded with you to make her your slave, hitch her to your plow, beat her, would that make it moral? If she asked you to help her commit suicide, would that make it moral? Can you treat another human being as a means? Think a minute: How much of what you say comes from a vested interest?

— *"Everybody on welfare cheats."*
     Always have an Almanac in the classroom; best book buy for seven bucks. Hand it to one student; don't just read it out. Okay, look up what you get for welfare per month for a family of four in this state. (In New York in 1991 it was $532.) Most families spend a quarter to a third of their budget on food. So divide that number by four. Now divide it by thirty days. Now divide it by four people. Now divide it by three meals. If you had thirty-seven cents for each of your kids per meal, would you cheat? What percentage of people on welfare are able-bodied? The government says fewer than ten percent. Should we take it away from people who would die without it? Who are the only people eligible for it? Look it up. The aged, the blind, the crippled, and children.

— *"Faith is a blind leap in the dark."*
     A blind leap into anything is sheer idiocy. If someone offered you five acres in Florida for $5,000, that's a blind leap in the dark. Nope. Faith is Greg Louganis. When he took that final dive after cracking his head, it was an act of faith —based on his previous experience and the advice of his coach. It was a leap, all right, but it wasn't blind. It was a *calculated* risk.

—*"Morality changes from age to age."*

That's why it's essential not to skip the epistemology class. Subjective morality surely changes from age to age, but objective morality doesn't. It's grounded in the very natures of things. Rocks are the same now as they were thousands of years ago. So are carrots and bunnies. So are human beings. Morality means humanity, and to say morality changes from age to age is to say humanity changes from age to age. If that were true, there'd be no need for libraries.

—*"Humans are only high-level animals."*

Pretty much the same question, and voiced from the same vested interest. Unfortunately, much of this reductionist thought comes from well-meaning science teachers, people who themselves are ardent Catholics. The pivotal argument against this statement is conscience. As far as we can tell, no tiger gobbles up a lamb and lurches back into the jungle saying, "My God, I've done it *again!* I've got to get counseling!" Humans do. At least good humans do. Bad humans don't.

—*"Gays choose to be homosexual."*

Absolutely false. Did you sit down one day, assess the advantages and disadvantages of heterosexuality, and choose it? No one chooses to be gay any more than they choose to be left-handed. This one is so deeply ingrained, especially in boys, that it's wise to bring a book with you (books tell the truth; teachers always have a hidden agenda). *New York Magazine* quotes Dr. C.A. Tripp, who interviewed over seven hundred homosexuals and scores of field anthropologists all over the world and draws several conclusions: 1. Sexual preferences are not hereditary or explicitly chosen; they are learned. A powerful homosexual conditioning begins at such an early age that the child is often more aware of pressures against heterosexuality than against homosexuality. 2. It has a higher ratio in macho and competitive societies (Greece, Rome, our own) and doesn't rise much above zero in societies that eschew heroics and thus take the glory out of maleness. 3. Only a fraction of homosexuals are effeminate. More than ninety percent show no effeminacy at all. Cf. NFL.

—*"Conscience is inborn."*

If that were true, how did we get Hitler? Each of us is born a little animal, the Id, but with the potential no animal has: to become humanized. Parents impose a Superego on that Id to keep you from getting hurt: a sort of temporary conscience till you can form one of your own, an Ego. If you're too busy to do that, you'll spend the rest of your life being jerked around by contradictory commands taped on a child's conscience.

—*"Nobody listens to the lyrics, just the music."*

Then if I give you a line, why can you give me the next five? Nobody listens to commercials either, right? Then why do very clever business people spend megabucks on them every year? The teacher should buy a few fanzines and do a survey, grouping the lyrics (at least the ones they can print) by theme, e.g., "Baby, it's all over but let's do it one more time." There's a message there, all right. And kids are caught between that omnipresent message and your message.

—*"You've gotta give 120 percent."*

Usually this is from boys, and it's usually about athletics not school, and it usually comes from someone with an A mind and a C+ average. Perfectionism works even for the ones who have settled for the "gentleman's 70"—simply because in the past they have tried and gotten little better than that. For them, perfect is impossible, so why try? One of the worst things parents can say to kids is, "If you applied yourself, you could be the top student in your year." No. Just better than now.

—*"So, if you cheat, who gets hurt?"*

Everybody, including you. For one thing, you make people who are trying to be honorable feel like damn fools, which is not exactly a lovable trait in you. For another, the teacher says, "Well, Sylvia Mugwump passed, so the quiz wasn't as hard as the better students say it was." But most important, you hurt yourself. You're a petty cheat. "No! I'm an honorable person who only cheats when she has need and opportunity."

But the problem is very real. This year I gave a survey in which one statement was: "If a friend copped the test beforehand, I wouldn't look at it." Only five out of sixty-three said they wouldn't. Be vigilant, but not just vigilant. Constantly try to find motives they will appreciate to be *honorable.* I had a surprising effect one day in class, quite by accident, when I was talking about narcissism. I said, "Would any *adult* cheat because he or she has need and opportunity? Would any adult copy a lab, lie to get out of a minor scrape, ask for an extension, put aside a necessary job because he or she wasn't in the mood? Would any adult? If you'd do that, routinely, then you're quite obviously not one of them." The faces looked knives at me. I had 'em!

—*"Love is a feeling totally uncapturable in words or concepts."*

Routinely, about half agree with that idiotic statement. It shows that they do, indeed, listen to the lyrics. There are no genuine "love songs," only "being-in-love songs." Love is not a feeling; love is an act of the will. Love takes over when the feelings fail, when the beloved is no longer even likable. I make them memorize that one. They may not accept it, but some day it might come in handy when they pick it up at the bottom of their memories.

— *"It's okay for us because we love one another."*
I thought I knew what real love meant when I was eighteen, too. Ten years later, what I'd known about love at eighteen was laughable. Now, forty years later, it's just sad. I was such a nice kid. And such a jerk about love. Ask your parents—in fact ask any adult you ride the bus with—if they really understood what love meant when they were your age. The result is guaranteed. Test me out. Now, why is it that, of all the people in this world, only you two know what love really means at eighteen?

You know what? What I do for you every day and every night is real loving: reading the reaction papers, grading the quizzes, being prepared every day, looking for gimmicks to hook your attention, putting up with the crap—and coming back for more! That's love.

And it is, you know.

Godspeed.